Annie Sloan's
Complete Book of
Decorative
Paint Finishes

Annie Sloan's

Complete Book of
Decorative
Paint Finishes

A step-by-step guide to mastering painting techniques for the home

Reader's Digest

THE READER'S DIGEST ASSOCIATION, INC.
Pleasantville, New York/Montreal

This edition published by The Reader's Digest Association
by arrangement with Collins & Brown Limited
Bramley Road
London W10 6SP

An imprint of **Chrysalis** Books Group plc

Conceived, edited and designed by Collins & Brown Limited

U.S. Project Editor: Barbara Booth
Canadian Project Editor: Pamela Johnson
Project Designer: George McKeon
Executive Editor, Trade Publishing: Dolores York
Associate Publisher, Trade Publishing: Christopher T. Reggio
Vice President & Publisher, Trade Publishing: Harold Clarke

Library of Congress Cataloging-in-Publication Data
Sloan, Annie, 1949-
    Annie Sloan's complete book of decorative paint finishes / Annie Sloan.
        p. cm.
    Includes index.
    ISBN 0-7621-0447-3
    1. House painting--Amateurs' manuals. 2. Furniture finishing–Amateurs'
    manuals. 3. Textile painting–Amateurs' manuals. 4. Decoupage–Amateurs'
    manuals. 5. Stencil work–Amateurs' manuals. I. Title: Complete book of
    decorative paint finishes. II. Title.

    TT305.S585 2004
    698'.14--dc22

Address any comments about the *Complete Book of Decorative Paint Finishes* to:
        The Reader's Digest Association, Inc.
        Adult Trade Publishing
        Reader's Digest Road
        Pleasantville, NY 10570-7000

For more Reader's Digest products and information, visit our website:
        www.rd.com (in the United States)
        www.readersdigest.ca (in Canada)

Reproduction by International Graphic Studios,
Midsomer Norton, UK
Printed and bound by Times Offset (M) Sdn. Bhd, Malaysia

1 3 5 7 9 10 8 6 4 2

Contents

Introduction

*A*NNIE *SLOAN'S COMPLETE BOOK OF DECORATIVE PAINT FINISHES* explores all the techniques you will ever need to decorate your home creatively, innovatively, and with professional results. Techniques

Paint Effects

So many effects and variations can be achieved using the same basic materials. The secret ingredient for all the effects is the glaze: a slow-drying, transparent medium that serves as the carrier for the color, whether paint or dry powder pigment. Unlike paint, which dries relatively quickly, glaze dries slowly, allowing you to continue working on a wet surface to produce a decorative finish. Using special brushes, sponges, and combs—or just everyday materials like rags and newspaper—you can create attractive patterns

combining base color and glaze color. Since it is transparent, the glaze gives an extra dimension to the paint, which remains more or less visible beneath, depending on the technique.

Although paint effects may look complicated, they are in fact very easy to do. All the techniques in this book have been carried out with water-based glazes, which are simpler to use than oil glazes, especially for the beginner. You can experiment with different mixes: more or less glaze with more or less color to give different degrees of opacity.

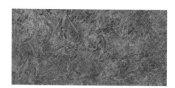

Ragging
Ragging (see pp. 20–23) is an adaptable technique that produces an irregular effect. Dab a cotton rag firmly onto wet glaze to reveal the base color in places. The effect is delicate when similar colors are used, and more lively when the contrast between the two—here, warm pink and mid-blue—is pronounced.

Sponging
Sponging (see pp. 24–27) is quick and easy to do and produces a regular, dappled effect. You can either sponge on your second color as here— a dark gray has been sponged onto a pale gray basecoat —or you can brush on the second color and then use a sponge to remove it in places.

Colorwashing
Colorwashing (see pp. 28–35) gives a carefree, natural look. By wiping gently over wet glaze with a soft cloth, you remove the brushmarks and give it a loose feel that works particularly well on walls. Choose colors quite close in tone, and use the darker one on top—here, warm yellow ocher on off-white.

Stippling
Stippling (see pp. 36–41) provides a very sophisticated, even effect, that from a distance can look untextured. It is most subtle when a lighter basecoat is covered by a darker shade of the same color.

from ragging and sponging to woodgraining and marbling, stenciling with brushes, rollers or spray paints, traditional and modern decoupage, staining wood, and distressing metal leaf are explained with step-by-step instructions and illustrated on walls, furniture, and accessories. Examples of how the effects look using different colors are also included, so that you can choose the perfect combinations for your project.

Combing

Combing (see pp. 42–47) creates a strong dramatic finish, since the comb concentrates the top color into lines, allowing the base color to show through clearly. This is most obvious when dark and light colors—here, dark blue on pale blue—are used in combination.

Dragging and Flogging

Dragging and flogging (see pp. 48–55) are developed from woodgraining techniques and, by using long, coarse-bristled brushes, produce a variegated, striped look. Flogging gives a more subtle look than dragging (shown here), but with both techniques the stripes are clearer the greater the color contrast between the basecoat and the glaze.

Patterning with Cloth

The soft, cloudy look is achieved by using cheesecloth/mutton cloth, a finely knitted cotton fabric (see pp. 56–59). A piece of the fabric is formed into a small pad and dabbed over the wet glaze. The fabric print leaves a deliberately uneven texture.

Rag Rolling

This effect (see pp. 60–63) uses two techniques: first the glaze is stippled; then, while it is still wet, a crumpled rag is rolled over the surface, removing some of the glaze to reveal the color beneath.

Frottage

Frottage (see pp. 64–69) is a French word meaning "rubbing." This is the only technique that does not use glaze. It is done using thinned-down paint over which an absorbent material such as newspaper or fabric is rubbed. Each new "rubbing" produces a different effect, making a random pattern.

Woodgraining

This is a traditional effect in which paint and glaze are used to imitate wood (see pp. 70–75). Techniques are shown for oak, mahogany, and maple graining—these can be adapted to reproduce other woods. Careful observation and accuracy are needed for successful results.

Decorative Graining

Decorative graining (see pp. 76–79) is a quick form of woodgraining, using a special tool to make lots of decorative effects, from obviously fake folk woodgraining to producing a finish like moiré or watered silk. Accurate imitation of wood is not the aim.

Marbling

Marbling (see pp. 80–89) is a very old technique and uses a combination of other basic techniques, such as sponging and ragging. A badger-hair brush is the essential tool, used to soften the glaze and give it the appearance of smooth marble.

Stencil Effects

Stenciling provides a customized way to apply patterns to walls, furniture, and fabrics. You can choose among a wide range of patterns and a virtually unlimited variety of styles.

Using Stencil Brushes

This most traditional type of stenciling (see pp. 100–105) can be used for all style designs, from Victorian to folk art, depending on the method and colors that you choose. You apply a small amount of paint with a short-bristled stencil brush, either by stippling, wiping, or swirling on the paint.

Using Rollers

This quick technique (see pp. 106–109) works especially well on walls and for large, open areas of stenciling. You coat a sponge roller with paint, wipe off the excess, then roll the paint over the stencil. The results vary from solid to lightly textured, depending on how hard and how many times you roll the paint on. This wall design —a pattern inspired by Chinese wallpaper—was rolled in blue over a creamy white.

Using Spray Paints

For fine, delicate, and intricate designs like this one, the spray technique (see pp.110–115) is the best choice. It results in a very even, finely dotted application of color. You can merge the dots for more solid coverage by using a greater amount of spray. Any of the spray paints sold for use by artists and model-makers or for vehicle spraying works well.

Decoupage

Decoupage is the art of cutting out paper designs and applying them to decorative objects, furniture, and walls. It was established in 18th-century France and Italy and by the 19th century had become a popular hobby for Victorian ladies. Today the technique can be used to mimic the traditional style or can take on many modern variations.

Preparing Motifs

You can use a sharp, pointed pair of scissors or a craft knife not only to cut with precision, but to cut imaginatively and thereby enhance your design (see pp. 124–127). Here, a small bunch of grapes was cut out of a larger grape design.

Staining and Coloring

Use watercolors, watersoluble pencils, inks, and teabags to color and stain black and white prints (see pp. 128–133). This motif was given a three-dimensional quality using shellac and pigments.

Gluing

You can also use glue creatively (see pp. 134–137). The flower stalk of this motif was bent to one side while the paper was wet with glue.

Varnishing and Finishing

The type of varnish you use (see pp. 138–145) can enhance the character of your design. Modern and traditional varnishes are used, as well as pigmented and scratched varnishes and aging techniques. Here, cracked varnish was used in places on this letter rack, resulting in a subtle finish.

Traditional Decoupage

One traditional method of decoupage (see pp. 146–149) is to position pictures, or scraps as they were known in the 19th century, close together and overlapping, to create scrap scenes on pieces of furniture (usually screens). This tray was decorated in that style, with overlapping figures and landscapes.

Decoupage on Glass

This technique involves positioning motifs behind glass (see pp. 150–157), which makes the decoupage look sharp and clear. Use pictures, silhouettes, or designs in tissue paper, as shown, to create stained-glass effects, with backdrops of paint, crackle paint, or metal leaf for added effect.

Decoupage with Freehand Painting
Freehand painting (see pp. 158–161) gives an added dimension to decoupage. Here, black and white fish motifs were enhanced with hand-painted lines and dots to create a water effect.

The Print Room
The print room combines prints with border frames, ribbons, swags, and chains (see pp. 162–167), usually on a wall. However, you can also use decorative detailing to adorn wastebaskets, like this one, and other small objects.

Making Your Own Designs
You can make your own designs using plain or store-bought patterned papers (see pp. 168–175). Use templates or cut symmetrical designs like the trees on the chest of drawers shown here.

Wood Finishes

Using paints, stains, waxes, and varnishes, you can decorate wood without losing the interest and beauty of its natural grain. A magnificent variety of woods are available, each exhibiting different types of grain—some smooth and narrow, some coarse and wide, some knotted, and others curled.

Using Homemade Stains
Homemade stains (see pp. 180–183) are simply made using basic materials such as pigments, Van Dyck crystals, and ferrous sulfate mixed with water. This headboard for a bed was partially stained using Van Dyck crystals, creating a dark brown stain.

Using Modern Stains
Modern stains (see pp. 184–189) come in premixed form so you can use them straight from the can. For pale, soft or bright colors on softwoods, you can use waterbased products. This tabletop was incised with a sharp knife and then stained with deep, strong, oil-base stains, which are more suitable for hardwoods.

Fuming and Bleaching

You can darken wood using the fumes from ammonia carbonate to give a piece an aged look, or lighten wood using a specialty two-part wood bleach. Fuming and bleaching are techniques used by the restorer, but you can also use them in a decorative way (see pp. 190–195). This block of wood shows its normal color in the middle with fumed and bleached corners above and below.

Penwork

You can contrast finely grained woods with a decoration in ink using the traditional technique of penwork (see pp. 196–199). You usually use India ink, which is black, or sepia drawing ink, but you can also use ordinary writing ink for a more transparent effect. The penwork on this panel was done in India ink inspired by an antique marquetry design.

Gilding

Long considered the domain of the specialist, gilding is in fact far simpler and has a far wider range of applications than those traditionally associated with it. Gilding involves a variety of techniques to revamp tired furniture, plain modern pieces, or even walls.

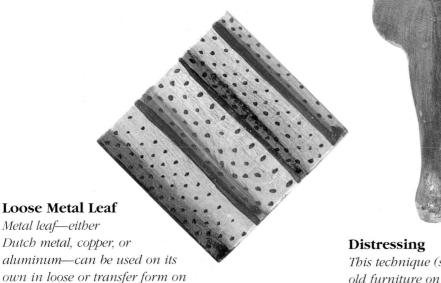

Loose Metal Leaf

Metal leaf—either Dutch metal, copper, or aluminum—can be used on its own in loose or transfer form on surfaces such as wood and plaster, or it may be used as a background. Paint is applied on top, as a wash or as an opaque coat, with a lot of the background uncovered. This technique (see pp. 206–209) works particularly well on small items.

Distressing

This technique (see pp. 210–213) re-creates the look of old furniture on which metal leaf has rubbed off over the years to reveal the basecoat below. These painted chair legs were covered in metal leaf and then distressed with steelwool. This breaks up the leaf into tiny pieces, leaving traces of metal on the painted surface. Distressing works best on furniture or frames.

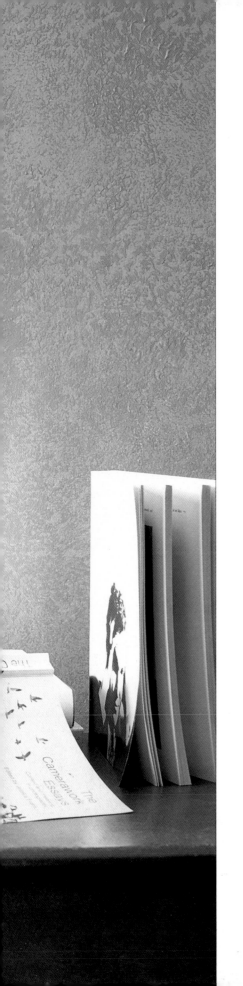

Paint Effects

The paint techniques in this chapter can be used to achieve many effects and variations with the same basic materials. Using special brushes, sponges and combs, or just everyday materials like rags and newspaper you can create attractive patterns combining base color and glaze color. Although paint effects may look complicated, you'll find they are very easy to do.

Preparing Surfaces

A NY SURFACE THAT CAN BE painted on can be given a special paint effect. The only constraint is that the surface should be a little porous and not too shiny. Glass and ceramics are difficult to paint on, but specialty products are available for this purpose. Rough wall surfaces – even brick, stone, unplaned wood, and textured wallpaper – can all be treated, provided an appropriate technique is chosen. However, a smooth surface offers the greatest choice of techniques and the best chance for a successful result. It is worth taking the time, therefore, to fill cracks in walls and strip and sand furniture carefully before painting.

Stripping Furniture

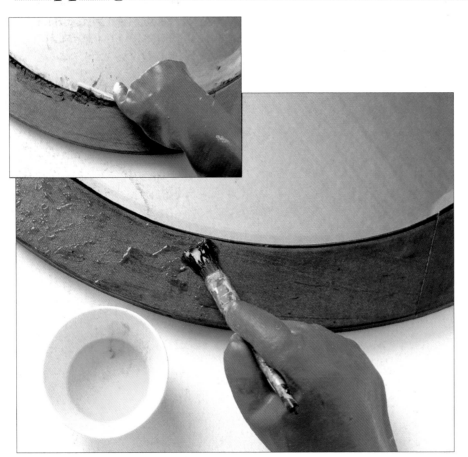

2 Remove the softened paint or varnish with coarse and then fine steel wool.

1 Old paint and varnish must be removed before painting furniture. Wearing rubber gloves, apply chemical stripper over the surface with a paintbrush. Use an old toothbrush to get into the crevices of carved or molded surfaces (inset). Leave the stripper on until the old coat has bubbled up.

3 Wipe off excess stripper with an absorbent cloth and the neutralizer recommended by your product. If you are applying water-base varnish, do not use turpentine or white spirit.

Filling Cracks

1 Using a sharp pointed tool such as a screwdriver, dig out the loose plaster from the crack.

2 Using a trowel, lay a generous amount of filler over the crack. Cover about 18in/45cm at a time.

3 With the flat edge of the trowel, work the filler into the crack, pulling the trowel down to make a smooth surface.

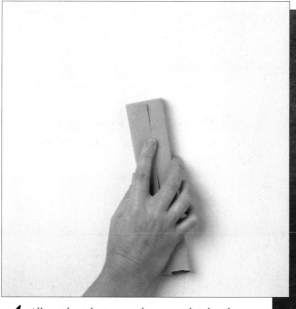

4 Allow the plaster to dry completely, then rub over the surface with fine-grade sandpaper wrapped around a block of wood (above). Once you have brushed off the dust left by sanding, apply the basecoat in preparation for the glaze (right). If the surface is still not smooth enough, sand it once again and apply another basecoat.

Basic Equipment

T HE BASIC TOOLS YOU NEED for glazing are the same as for any painting job: drop cloths/dust sheets for protecting floors and furniture, rags for wiping up spills, and rollers and brushes of different sizes for applying the basecoat and glaze. (Specialty brushes are recommended for individual techniques; these are shown on the relevant pages.) For typical painting tasks, the paint you buy is ready-mixed. When glazing, it can be useful to have an assortment of bowls and basins for mixing and experimenting with different colors.

Applying the Basecoat

Rollers allow you to apply paint quickly over a large flat area, but they leave a fine "orange peel" texture, which you may not want for the final basecoat. For the best results apply the final coat with a brush. Stippling and patterning with cloth, in particular, need a very smooth, even surface. Special brushes are not required; just use one that feels comfortable.

Mohair roller

Fine sponge roller

Smaller brushes for intricate areas and corners

Wide flat brushes for covering large areas

Applying Glaze

Use flat-ended brushes for applying oil-base glaze and oval-shaped for applying water-base glaze. Several widths of brush may be needed, depending on the size of the surface being covered.

Oval-shaped brushes for applying water-base glaze

Artist's fitch for painting intricate areas

Flat-ended brushes for applying oil-base glaze

Other Equipment

You will need extra equipment for preparing your glazes and keeping surfaces clean. A plastic bucket or bowl is useful for mixing glazes and glaze colors, and a glass jar is ideal for mixing oil glaze and pigment to the proper consistency. Use a drop cloth or dust sheet to protect the surfaces you do not want paint or glaze to spill on, and a piece of cloth is useful for wiping surfaces clean and removing excess glaze.

Rags for wiping up spills

Plastic paint bucket for mixing glaze

Thin brush for mixing and painting

Bowl for mixing glaze colors

Glass jar

Drop cloth/dust sheet

Using Glazes

T HE AMOUNT OF PAINT or coloring agent that you mix in with your glaze depends on how opaque you want your glaze to be. The more paint you add the more opaque the effect will be. With normal water-base glaze you should mix four to six parts glaze to one part paint. Remember that the more paint there is, the quicker it dries, leaving less time to complete your effect.

Your prime concern is that the glaze does not dry out before you complete your effect. If glazing a large area, apply the glaze in sections for certain techniques and in strips for others.

Levels of Opacity

Glaze can have either a lot or a little paint mixed with it. The more paint is added the more opaque the effect. Here, a green glaze was applied over a blue ragged background. On the left it was simply painted on, while on the right it was also ragged. The progression from top to bottom shows that when more and more paint is added, the background blue is obliterated.

Painting in Sections

1 *For ragging, sponging, stippling, colorwashing, patterning with cloth, and some combing techniques, apply the glaze over an area about 18in/45cm square.*

2 *Carry out the required technique on the glaze, leave an unworked strip on one side, known as the* wet edge. *Paint the next area of glaze right into this so that a line is not created where the two sections meet.*

Painting in Strips

1 *For dragging, flogging, and some combing techniques, apply the glaze in a strip from ceiling to molding. Drag, flog, or comb down, leaving a wet edge so the next strip can be joined invisibly. Wipe off any glaze that has spread onto the molding.*

2 *Drag or flog from the bottom of the wall by drawing the brush upward. This helps to break up the brushmarks and to avoid a build-up of glaze at the edge.*

GLAZING ON RAISED SURFACES

Paint effects also work well on rough or irregular surfaces, such as raised wallpaper. You can either choose a technique to mask the texture or to accentuate it. As a general rule, choose an effect that produces an irregular, highly patterned surface, such as ragging, to disguise a pattern and a plain, smooth effect, such as colorwashing, will enhance it. However, this does depend on the pattern you are glazing over. You can see how the pattern on the wallpaper below is far more noticeable after it has been dragged as opposed to stippled, since the basecoat shows through, emphasizing the pattern on the dragging.

Dragging

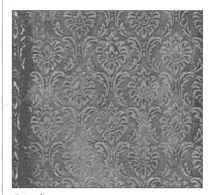

Stippling

Ragging

Ragged Wall

A yellow-ocher glaze, darkened with a hint of terra-cotta red, was ragged over an off-white background. When choosing the color combinations for your wall, avoid highly contrasting colors unless you want a very dramatic effect.

Ragging produces a lively irregular pattern that is suitable for decorating both walls and pieces of furniture. You bunch a rag the size of a large napkin in your hand and then dab it firmly onto the wet glaze, so that it removes the glaze in parts, revealing the base color underneath. A soft cotton rag is most commonly used, but different materials make different patterns, depending on their thickness and absorbency – heavy linen, for instance, makes a bold, crisp effect, while polyester cloth gives a lighter, more undefined look.

The color of the basecoat is vital in ragging because so much of it is revealed. The standard style is to cover it with a glaze a few tones darker – the more similar the colors are, the subtler the effect.

TOOLS & MATERIALS

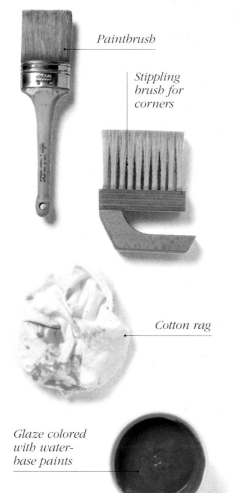

Paintbrush

Stippling brush for corners

Cotton rag

Glaze colored with water-base paints

The Basic Technique

1 Apply a liberal coat of glaze over a maximum area of 20 in/130 cm square, using criss-cross brushstrokes.

2 Dab a bunched-up rag over the wet glaze to lift it off. Leave a strip unragged along the edges.

3 After about 10 dabs, re-form the rag so it doesn't become saturated. When the whole rag is sodden, replace it with a new one.

4 Repeat Steps 1 and 2 until you have covered the whole surface.

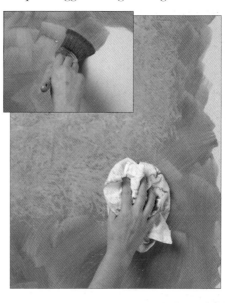

Avoiding Glaze Build-up in Corners

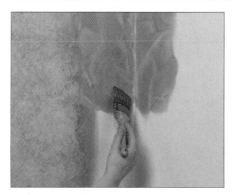

1 Apply glaze to the surface in the same way as in The Basic Technique, *but be careful so it's not too thick in the corner.*

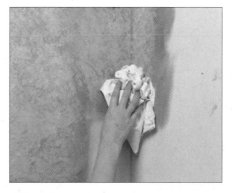

2 Dab the rag gently into the corner, applying more pressure to one side than the other to prevent the glaze from being smeared.

3 When the glaze is nearly dry – after about half an hour – dab firmly into the corner with a stippling brush to remove any excess glaze.

Special Effects

It is usual to rag until the brushmarks are no longer visible. But you can make a special feature of them by leaving parts of the surface unragged.

Over small areas, such as panels, you can make a pattern by dabbing at regular intervals while keeping the rag in the same position in your hand.

Double Ragging

When the glaze is dry, you layer in a different color, or a deeper shade of the same color, to intensify the effect. This also lets you adjust a color that is not quite right.

PITFALLS
A layer of glaze that is too thick results in a glutinous and bubbly surface (below). A layer of glaze that is spread too far or made with only a little paint will make a weak effect when ragged (bottom).

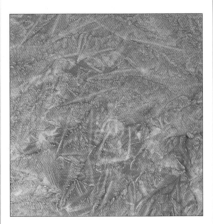

Glaze too thick

Glaze too thin

Ragged Frame
LEFT This frame was covered with a coat of cool gray-blue and then ragged over with a warm chocolate-brown glaze.

Double-Ragged Box
BELOW The yellow ocher basecoat on this box was ragged over twice in a dark red to give a greater intensity of color.

Ragged Candlestick
LEFT The dark, subtle effect on this candlestick was achieved by ragging a rich, clear blue over a brown basecoat.

COLOR COMBINATIONS

Dark red on light gray

Dark green on paler green

Yellow ocher on terra-cotta red

Dark blue on off-white

RAGGING WITH OTHER MATERIALS

Plastic wrap and other types of plastic give a strong, clearly defined pattern that works well on furniture. If you use it on walls, keep the colors close in tone to stop the effect from being overwhelming. Paper towel works well on all surfaces. It gives a soft, slightly spotted finish.

Plastic wrap

Paper towel

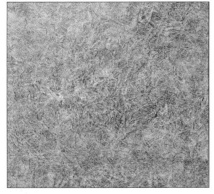

Using plastic wrap

Using paper towel

Sponging

Sponged Tabletop

The deep, rich color of this tabletop was achieved by sponging several shades of turquoise together with a little brighter green for contrast over a black basecoat. Layers were built up for a dense effect.

SPONGING PRODUCES a lively, informal effect that can be achieved in two different ways. Both are quick and easy to do. You can apply colored glaze with a brush over the basecoat – which can be either darker or lighter in tone – and then partially remove it with a sponge. This is called "sponging off." Or, the glaze can be applied directly with a sponge, called "sponging on." A natural sea sponge gives good results by making small, irregular spots of color. Sponging off creates a denser effect, while sponging on gives a lighter look. Responging with other colors gives greater depth.

Sponging on can be done just using paint without mixing in a glaze, especially on small areas, but the use of glaze helps to build up translucent layers of color, adding to the impression of depth.

TOOLS & MATERIALS

*Brush for
applying glaze*

*Large
sponge*

*Small sponge
for sponging
in corners*

Blue glaze

The Basic Technique

1 Generously paint on the colored glaze. The brushstrokes can be uneven, but the background surface should be well covered.

2 With a damp sponge, dab all over the glaze, pressing firmly to disguise any brushstrokes. Change the angle of your wrist to avoid a regular pattern. Leave a wet edge.

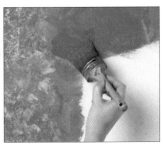

3 Again using a brush, work into the wet edge, applying a generous amount of glaze for the next section.

4 Continue as before, sponging over the brushstrokes. Rinse the sponge in a bucket of water when it has absorbed a lot of glaze, squeezing out well.

Sponging a Corner

1 Brush the glaze on both walls and into the corner, working it in well. Dab off the glaze from the walls as explained in The Basic Technique.

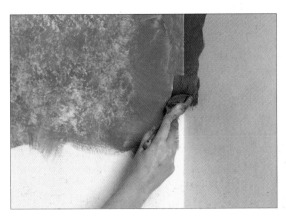

2 In order to dab right into the corner, use a small sponge or break off a piece of the large sponge.

Double Sponging

You can achieve interesting effects by building up layers of different colors. Dab on colors next to each other or overlap them to produce a third color. Sponging on and sponging off can also be mixed. Sponging off often gives a more solid base, over which you can sponge on other colors or tones to create depth and highlights. Or, sponge on several colors to give a subtly flecked effect.

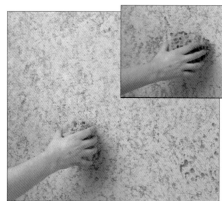

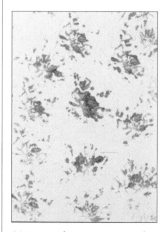

1 *Use two, three, four, or more colors to build up density. Here, the first color is applied lightly, letting the background show through.*

2 *The second and third layers of glaze, in dark red and pale yellow, are applied. The previous layer may be slightly wet, but if you make a mistake you will have to start again.*

3 *The final layer, dark blue-gray glaze, is applied. Painting on a layer of varnish between layers protects previous work if you have to wipe off or reapply glaze.*

Using Synthetic Sponges

Using rectangular synthetic sponges gives a very different result from natural sponges. Here, a deliberately hard-edged effect is created using different sized sponges with two colors of glaze.

PITFALLS

Sponging on is less successful if the glaze color contrasts too much with the color of the basecoat (below left). Also, if the sponging is too far apart – leaving large gaps – the effect is patchy. Sponging off looks heavy and coarse if the glaze is too thick and dark (below right).

Too much contrast and too far apart

Glaze too thick

Sponged Wall

ABOVE A pink-toned terra-cotta glaze was applied with a brush over an off-white basecoat. The glaze was then sponged off to produce an evenly dappled effect.

Sponged Candlestick

RIGHT The stone effect on this candlestick was achieved by sponging on shades of ocher, gray, and dark cream irregularly over a cream base.

COLOR COMBINATIONS

Dark green, then khaki, on pale olive green

Black on bright blue

Yellow ocher on deep red

Striped Wall

ABOVE Blue and white stripes were painted on the wall with a roller. Pale blue was sponged over the blue and a darker blue over the white.

Sponged Chair

ABOVE The chair was first painted blue; then reds and yellows were sponged on the seat and back slats.

Deep red on bright green

Colorwashing

HIS TECHNIQUE RESULTS in different characteristics, depending on the colors you use. With earthy ochers the effect is reminiscent of an old lime-washed wall with contrasting dark and faded patches. With strong, rich colors, such as crimson or emerald green, the result is like oriental lacquer, especially when enhanced with a coat of gloss or satin varnish. Soft pastel colors look best either left natural or with a coat of flat varnish. Unlike other paint techniques, which are carried out in strips or patches, you can cover a large surface area with glaze all at once because, when colorwashing, you only wipe or brush off the glaze when it is nearly dry to avoid leaving scratch marks. If the glaze dries out too much you can use a lightly dampened cloth.

Colorwashed Fireplace

The simple shape of this fireplace was given interest by subtle colorwashing. Over a basecoat of pale blue-gray, glazes of blue, mahogany red, and a dark mixture of the two were applied in patches of varying intensity. The glazes were lightly wiped over, allowed to dry, then reapplied to strengthen the depth of color. The sides of the mantel shelf and edges of the side panels were wiped off with a soft cloth while the glaze was still wet to create a contrasting border.

COLORWASHING IN CLOSE-UP

This detail shows the contrast between the colorwashed effect built up in several layers and the paler edges where the top layers of glaze have been wiped off.

TOOLS & MATERIALS

Paintbrush for applying glaze

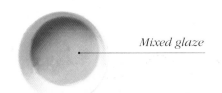

Smaller brush for corners and edges

Cheesecloth/ mutton cloth

Mixed glaze

The Basic Technique

1 Paint the glaze over the whole area to be covered and allow it to dry until it can be worked on without scratching the glaze. If the area is too large the glaze may dry too quickly, so work in patches, leaving a wet edge to work into.

2 Wipe over the wall with a soft cloth, using strokes of different lengths in all directions. Press hard enough to expose the basecoat but not to remove all the glaze.

3 The cloth will become saturated with glaze as you work, so refold it and begin wiping again with a fresh section of cloth.

4 Continue smoothing out the glaze with the cloth until all the brushmarks are hidden and the color is evenly spread.

Colorwashing Above a Dado Rail

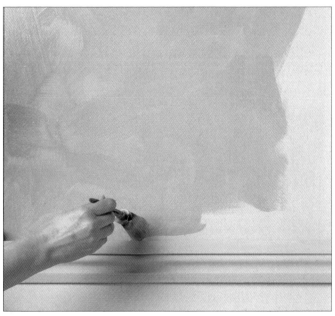

1 Using a 3 in/75 mm paintbrush, apply a generous layer of glaze to the area of the wall above the dado rail, taking care not to come too close to the dado rail itself.

2 Using a smaller brush (here, 1½ in/38 mm), apply the glaze carefully right up to the edge of the rail. Do not overload the brush.

4 Using a small cloth pad, wipe off any excess glaze in the recess between rail and wall.

3 When the glaze is almost dry, wipe it off in all directions using a soft cloth (see The Basic Technique, p. 29, Steps 2–4).

Double Colorwashing

A second layer of glaze in a different color, or in different shade of the first color, can be applied to intensify, deepen or lighten the first layer. The bigger the contrast between the two colors you choose, the more distinct the effect, since when the second glaze layer is wiped off, the background color will show through. To alter the look further, you can then apply more layers if desired.

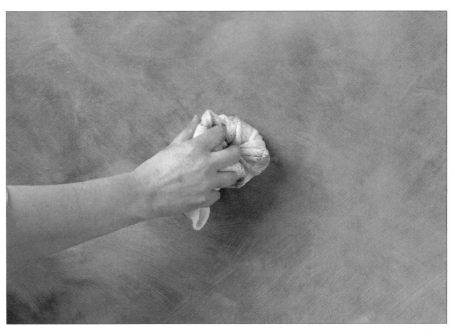

1 *Brush on the second layer of glaze (here, reddish brown) when the first layer (here, pale yellow ocher) is dry (see* The Basic Technique, *p. 29).*

2 *When the surface is nearly dry, wipe over it with a soft rag, removing some of the second layer and allowing the first color to show through.*

Colorwashing a Cornice

1 *This technique suits any carved or molded surface. Using a color a few tones darker than the basecoat, paint the glaze on with a small brush, working it well into the crevices.*

2 *When the glaze is nearly dry, wipe gently over the molded surface with a soft cloth. You may need to apply more pressure in certain areas to get an even look.*

Colorwashing a Carved Object

Colorwashing can be used to emphasize the depth of carving and molding. The darker colored glaze or paint accumulates in the crevices but is wiped off the raised areas, which, being lighter, then appear more prominent. This technique gives a pleasantly "aged" look to a new object such as the plaque shown here, as the darker color resembles dirt that has built up in the crevices over the years.

1 *For a denser effect use paint rather than glaze. Having painted on the basecoat (here, deep terra-cotta) and varnished it to prevent the second coat from being absorbed by the plaster of the plaque, paint on the second coat (here, brown-black).*

2 *When the paint is nearly dry, gently wipe a soft cloth over the face, using more pressure on the raised surfaces to remove more of the darker paint and to highlight the molding.*

3 *If the paint has dried or more needs to be removed, wipe over the raised areas with a lightly dampened cloth.*

The Finished Plaque
RIGHT The contrast between the lighter and darker areas on the finished plaque gives a convincing antique effect.

Using More than Two Colors

1 *You can apply more than two colors side by side, rather than overlaying them as in double colorwashing. First paint on patches of glaze (here, green), leaving spaces for the next color.*

2 *Cover all the empty areas with another layer of glaze in a color of similar intensity (here, light blue). To give strength and contrast, also dab on small patches of paint in a third color (here, dark blue).*

3 *Brush out the paint thoroughly to merge the darker color into the glaze. The colors should flow into each other, without any harsh edges.*

4 *Wipe all over the surface with a soft cloth in a circular polishing motion, smoothing out the colors. The result should be a soft, cloudy effect.*

COLORWASHING WITH BRUSHES
You can use brushes instead of a cloth to wipe off the glaze; this gives a coarser effect, showing the marks of the bristles. For a softer look, hold the tip of the brush at right angles to the surface and wipe gently as with a cloth. A soft wallpaper brush leaves less distinct lines than a hard brush.

Wallpapering brush

House painter's brush

Colorwashing with a soft brush

Colorwashing with a hard brush

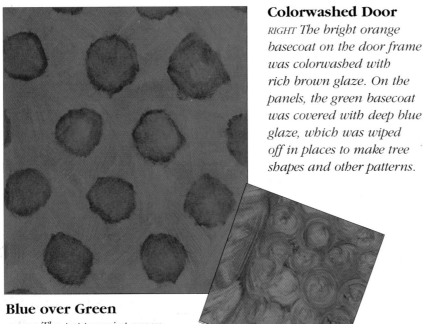

Colorwashed Door

RIGHT The bright orange basecoat on the door frame was colorwashed with rich brown glaze. On the panels, the green basecoat was covered with deep blue glaze, which was wiped off in places to make tree shapes and other patterns.

Blue over Green

ABOVE The peppermint green basecoat was colorwashed with sage green glaze. When dry, spots of blue glaze were dabbed on and the center of each was immediately wiped off lightly.

Terra-cotta over Orange

ABOVE A terra-cotta glaze was brushed over an orange basecoat. This was wiped off by twisting a cloth to create swirls.

Rustic Letter Rack

LEFT This look was created by colorwashing a clear middle-blue glaze over a bright yellow basecoat.

PITFALLS

Colorwashing is usually done by wiping off the glaze in all directions. If you wipe it off in one direction – here, diagonally (near right) – it looks less even. To achieve depth of color, it is better to apply two thin layers of glaze. If you apply one thick one the effect looks too heavy (far right).

Wiping off in one direction

Glaze too thick

Classical Plaque

RIGHT The plaque was covered with a coat of light gray-brown paint; then a dark glaze made from several shades of brown was painted over it. The surface was wiped over lightly to remove the glaze from the raised areas.

COLOR COMBINATIONS

Dark blue-green on bright green

Brown/mauve on beige

Yellow ocher on warm cream

Middle-blue on pale blue

Colorwashing with a Dado Rail

LEFT The muddy pink basecoat on this wall was colorwashed with dark crimson red glaze above the rail. Below it, the same glaze was used, with a little chocolate brown added.

Colorwashing with a Cornice

LEFT The wall beneath the white cornice has been colorwashed very simply with one layer of raw sienna over an off-white basecoat.

Stippling

Stippled Plaque and Wall

Both the wall and the plaque have been stippled with a green glaze so that they harmonize with each other even though the base colors are completely different. The wall was painted bright lemon yellow while the basecoat on the plaque is gray.

THIS CLASSIC TECHNIQUE gives a delicate, sophisticated effect. A thin, almost translucent layer of glaze is applied over the basecoat and hit with a special brush while still wet. The brush breaks up the glaze into small spots – though these can only be seen from close up – allowing the base color to show through. When choosing your colors, make sure that the glaze contains a high concentration of color since it needs to be spread very thinly. Use a white basecoat to show off primary colors, but for more muted shades, off-white may be more suitable. Colored bases will give richer, more complex finishes. Whatever colors you use, stippling works best on very smooth surfaces since it shows up every bump and imperfection.

TOOLS & MATERIALS

Mixed glaze and brush

3 x 4in/75 x 100mm stippling brush for small areas

1 x 4in/25 x 100mm stippling brush for corners and details

5 x 7in/127 x 178mm stippling brush for larger surfaces

The Basic Technique

1 Cover the surface with a layer of glaze, brushing it in all directions to spread it out very thinly.

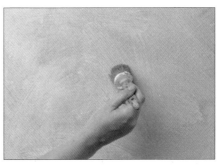

2 Go over the surface gently with the tip of the brush to make it as smooth and even as possible and to remove any brushmarks.

3 Using a large stippling brush, hit the surface with a steady, strong motion. Move on to the next area, repeating the action and overlapping the previous area each time. The finished effect should be evenly and finely speckled.

Dealing with Specks

1 Small blobs or specks of glaze are sometimes left from stippling. Remove these with your finger and stipple again immediately.

2 Wipe the stippling brush regularly with a cloth to remove the glaze that will accumulate on the bristles. Excess glaze on the brush will spoil the even effect you are aiming for.

Stippling a Corner

1 *Stipple up to the corner then using a small brush, paint the glaze right into the corner.*

2 *Stipple one wall as far into the corner as possible without hitting the other wall.*

3 *Stipple the other wall in the same way. Keep the bristles of the brush parallel to the surface of the wall and wipe off excess glaze from the brush as you work.*

4 *Using the smallest size stippling brush – 1 x 4in/25 x 100mm – stipple right into the corner, wiping off excess glaze. If you find that too much glaze is being removed, allow the glaze to dry a little before continuing.*

Stippling from Light to Dark

1 *First apply a band of the lightest colored glaze over the surface, spreading it out thinly and evenly (see* The Basic Technique, *p. 37, Steps 1–2).*

2 *Leaving a gap below the first band – here 2–3in/ 5–7.5cm – apply another band of the same color in the same way as in Step 1.*

3 While the second (lower) band is still wet, cover it with a second coat of glaze in the darker colored glaze, spreading it out evenly and thinly.

4 Brush the glaze out over the gap to join the darker color to the lighter color above it. Brush well over the edges so that the shades merge. Repeat Steps 2–4 using two layers of the darker colored glaze.

5 Stipple the whole area as directed in The Basic Technique (*see p. 37*), starting at the top in the lightest area and working downward into the darkest area. Working in this direction ensures that you do not take more glaze back into the paler area. When you have finished (right), the different colored bands should be barely perceptible, with the color just gradually becoming darker towards the bottom.

Stippling a Dado Rail

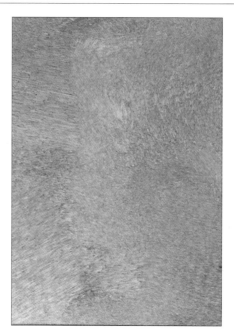

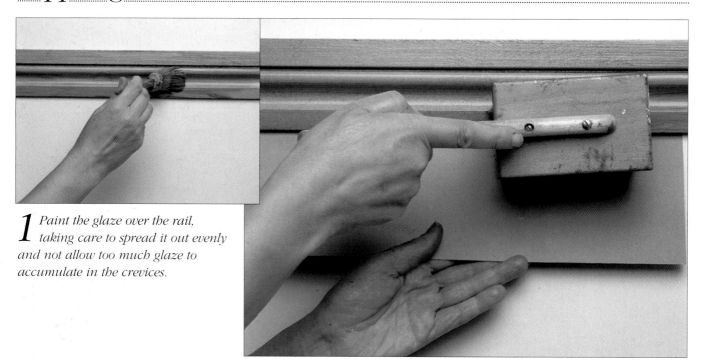

1 Paint the glaze over the rail, taking care to spread it out evenly and not allow too much glaze to accumulate in the crevices.

2 Using a smaller stippling brush – here 3 x 4in/75 x 100mm – stipple evenly along the surface, changing the angle at which you direct the brush to avoid brush-marks. Hold a piece of cardboard against the edge of the rail to protect the wall above and below.

PITFALLS

If you hit the stippling brush too hard on the surface you will create small lines and stripes (near right). Although this is not the classic effect, it could be used as a deliberate technique in itself. If the stippling brush is not hit hard enough against the surface (far right), the brush-marks of the original glaze application will be visible and you will not achieve a satisfactory stippled effect.

Hitting too hard

Hitting too lightly

Lamp Base

LEFT *This white lamp base was stippled with blue glaze mixed with a little white to lighten it. To get an even finish, you need to stipple the surface delicately and steadily while gradually rotating the lamp base.*

Stippled desk

LEFT AND ABOVE *The dense, velvety texture on this desk was achieved by stippling a cool shade of brown over the warm yellow ocher basecoat. This calm combination suggests natural wood grain.*

STIPPLING WITH OTHER BRUSHES

Any brush with short, rigid bristles can be used for stippling with less perfect, but still interesting results. The clusters of bristles in a dustpan brush, for example, leave a noticeable pattern (right).

Clothes brush

Dustpan brush

Stippling with a dustpan brush

COLOR COMBINATIONS

Blue on pink

Middle-blue on pale lemon

Red terra-cotta on orange

Dark green on middle-green

Combing

COMBS WERE ORIGINALLY USED for some types of woodgraining, but today are used for many other decorative effects, such as making stripes, checks, and borders. Traditional and contemporary sources can both provide inspiration: tartans, ginghams, madras plaids, and Regency stripes can all suggest stunning color combinations. When combing, the colors you use are more crucial than in other paint effects, which rely on the translucency of the glaze to enhance and deepen the base color. The glaze should be almost completely opaque when combing so that the lines that are created are clear and strong.

Tartan Table

The table was first painted red. When the paint was dry, broad stripes of green glaze were painted across the width of the table and combed with a graduated comb (see Tools & Materials, p. 43*). When this coat dried, rich blue stripes were painted on in the opposite direction and combed in the same way. Regularly spaced fine lines in pale yellow were painted on to complete the tartan effect.*

TOOLS & MATERIALS

Triangular comb with three different widths of teeth

Graduated comb with two widths of teeth

Glaze

Glazing brush

Rag for wiping glaze off combs

The Basic Technique

1 *Paint glaze over the area to be combed, making it as even as possible. If combing a wall, cover an area approximately 3 feet (1 meter) wide, from ceiling to floor.*

2 *Holding the comb in both hands, with the teeth slanted upward, pull it down carefully from the top. Do it quite quickly to avoid wobbles.*

3 *If you need to stop halfway, avoid making horizontal lines by lightly relaxing the pressure on the surface before removing the comb.*

Double Combing

Homemade and store-bought combs (see p. 44) offer teeth with varying widths, both regular and graduated. The possibilities they provide when used in double, triple, or even more layers produce an unlimited variety of combed stripes and checks. Try light, bright colors over dark colors, and vice versa. Below, a graduated comb is used twice to make a checkered pattern.

1 *Once the previously combed surface has dried completely, cover it with a different colored glaze, spreading it out as evenly as possible.*

2 *Comb across horizontally. Position yourself for maximum stabilty and hold the comb in both hands.*

Making a Comb

While it is possible to buy long-lasting, strong but supple combs, these may not be exactly the right size for your project. You can easily make your own combs using strong cardboard, but they will not last long, since the paper softens and absorbs paint. Soft plastic floor tiles are excellent for homemade combs since they are easy to cut but durable.

1 *Cut a rectangular shape in a flexible plastic floor tile. Mark the edge at regular intervals according to the width of tooth and spacing you want.*

2 *Draw a pencil line parallel to the edge and then draw "V" shapes between every second mark with the base of the "V" facing inward.*

3 *Carefully cut out the "V" shapes with a sharp knife, leaving blunted teeth.*

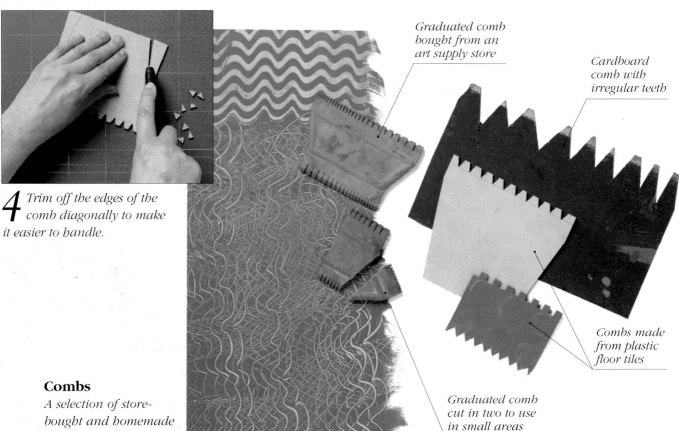

4 *Trim off the edges of the comb diagonally to make it easier to handle.*

Combs
A selection of store-bought and homemade combs in different materials and sizes.

Graduated comb bought from an art supply store

Cardboard comb with irregular teeth

Combs made from plastic floor tiles

Graduated comb cut in two to use in small areas

Checkerboard Combing

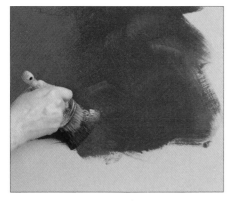

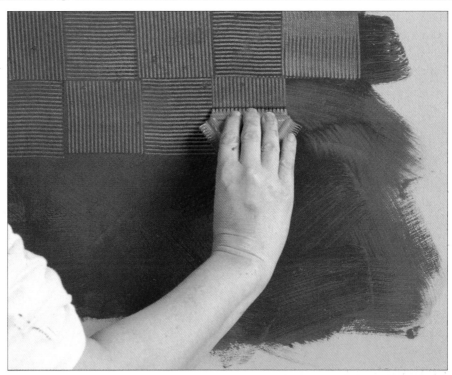

1 Apply the glaze with a brush,
spreading it out well. The glaze
should contain enough paint to
make it opaque.

2 Using a comb with broad,
regularly spaced teeth, make
alternate vertically and horizontally
combed squares (right).

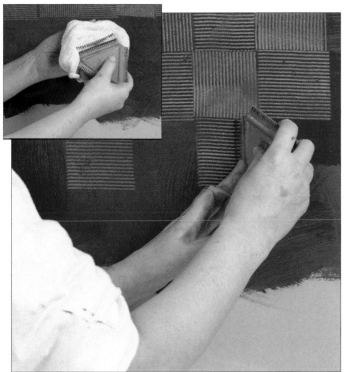

3 Wipe off excess glaze at frequent intervals. After a
couple of rows you may find it easier and quicker
to comb all the horizontal squares in a row, leaving
gaps between them.

4 Complete the pattern by combing vertical squares in
the remaining gaps. Instead of squares you could also
make diamond shapes by using the comb diagonally.

Alternatives

A vast range of effects can be produced by combing. The size of teeth, direction of the strokes, and color combinations can all be varied with interesting results.

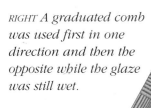

RIGHT A graduated comb was used first in one direction and then the opposite while the glaze was still wet.

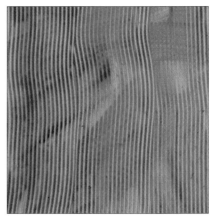

ABOVE Different effects were obtained on this blue glaze over a white basecoat, using combs with different size teeth.

ABOVE Green glaze was painted and combed over a red background. When dry, bright blue was combed across in the opposite direction.

LEFT Brown glaze on off-white was combed in a random criss-cross way on the top part of the wall. Underneath, bright blue glaze on terra-cotta was combed leaving regular gaps.

PITFALLS

The right consistency of glaze is critical for achieving the characteristic sharp contrast and smooth lines of combing. If the glaze is too thick (near right), the lines will be blurred, indistinct, and form ridges; if it is too thin (far right), the effect will be thin and watery. To check the consistency of glaze, practice on a small area first.

Glaze too thick

Glaze too thin

COLOR COMBINATIONS

Dark brown on bright green

Bright red on dark blue

White on bright blue

Light gray-green on dark green

Blue and Yellow Table

TOP, ABOVE AND RIGHT This small table was combed with several patterns to give a lively effect. Yellow glaze was applied in selected areas over blue paint and each leg was given a different treatment. A large area on top was left unglazed to heighten the impact of the combed pattern.

Chest of Drawers

LEFT A small drawer unit was painted all over in deep blue-black. White glaze was painted on the drawers and combed with a homemade comb the same width as the drawers. Alternate drawers were combed again to make a strong but irregular vertical stripe. On the remaining drawers the first layer was left to dry, and a second layer of white glaze was combed on horizontally to make a checkered pattern.

Wooden Chest

LEFT A simple wooden chest was painted soft mauve, then combed over with a graduated comb in a darker brown-purple. The subtle effect suggests woodgraining.

Dragging & Flogging

DRAGGING AND FLOGGING ARE two techniques that derive from wood-graining. They replicate this effect when carried out in appropriate wood-toned colors. When used with more varied colors they are decorative techniques in their own right, traditionally used on both plaster walls and woodwork. Historically, dragging was used from the ceiling to the dado rail, with marbled or stippled panels below. There is a subtle difference between the two finishes: dragging produces smooth stripes, while the flogging breaks up the stripes and creates a more uniform overall effect.

Kitchen Cupboard

Contrasting colors and techniques were used to decorate this simple kitchen cupboard. The top drawer front and door panels were painted light blue. Green glaze was dragged over this along the longest dimension. When dry, a second layer of the same green glaze was dragged at right angles to the first stripe. The remaining areas were painted middle-blue and darker blue glaze was dragged over it.

DRAGGING IN CLOSE-UP

Dragging uses a long, coarse-bristled brush and produces a pattern of broken stripes of different lengths. Brush widths range from 2½ to 12 in/62½ to 300 mm. Dragging on plaster walls is done vertically, but on wood it should follow the grain.

TOOLS & MATERIALS

Glaze brush

Dragging brush

Cloth for wiping off glaze

Mixed glaze

The Basic Technique: Dragging

1 Paint on the glaze, spreading it out evenly. Paint vertically in strips to obtain uniform coverage.

3 Using the dragging brush, draw the brush up and down, holding it almost parallel to the surface. This will give an even, vertical stripe. The effect should be smooth and without ridges. Leave a wet edge to work into later.

2 Brush out the glaze as much as possible to create a thin glaze layer. The surface should not feel sticky.

4 To soften the effect hold the brush at almost 90 degrees to the surface and brush up and down at a slight angle to the stripes.

5 Continue on the next strip, working the glaze into the previous wet edge and repeat Steps 3–4 until you have covered the whole surface.

Dragging a Door

Treat the parts of the door in the order they are numbered above. Always drag in the same direction as the grain of the wood.

1 Start applying the glaze in the top center stile (number 1 on the door). Stiles are vertical and rails horizontal.

2 Thoroughly spread out the glaze as evenly as possible, for a smooth and uniform coverage.

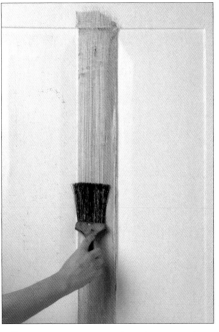

3 With a dragging brush, drag the glaze down over the whole top center stile and onto the rail.

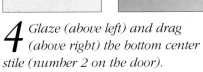

4 Glaze (above left) and drag (above right) the bottom center stile (number 2 on the door).

6 *Finally treat the two outer stiles (numbers 6 and 7), which extend the whole length of the door, making a neat join with the rails.*

5 *Starting at the top of the door, paint the glaze horizontally on the rails (numbers 3, 4, and 5) then drag across. Take care to leave a neat edge against the already dragged stiles.*

Dragging Below a Cornice

1 *When applying the glaze, leave an unglazed gap at the top of the wall near the cornice so the glaze will not be too heavy at this spot. Spread out the glaze vertically with the dragging brush.*

2 *Having wiped excess glaze off the brush on a paper towel (inset), hold the brush against the wall just below the cornice or rail, and apply a little pressure to the tip with the edge of your hand. This will release enough glaze to spread up to the top of the wall.*

Dragging with a Cloth

1 *Paint a contrasting glaze on the surface where a base color has already been applied.*

2 *Pull a bunched-up soft cloth across the surface in a straight line without stopping in the middle.*

Cloth Dragged Table

ABOVE This alternative method of dragging gives a very soft effect. It may be difficult to keep the lines straight, but aligning them visually with an edge and always working in the same direction will help.

Dragging with a Flogging Brush

A flogging brush is used in the same way as the dragging brush but produces a more pronounced striped effect. This can be particularly effective on furniture, and where the colors chosen are close in tone.

PITFALLS

When insufficient pressure is applied to the brush you will not achieve evenly striped dragging and the glaze will be patchy. If you bend your arm as you pull the brush down you will create a curved stroke. To avoid this, make shorter strokes so you can keep your arm straight. Mentally align the brush itself with a straight edge, rather than watching the mark left by it.

Not enough pressure

Curved stripes

COLOR COMBINATIONS

Dark green on bright green

Terra-cotta on bright pink

Off-white on varnished wood

Black on bright red

Chest of Drawers

ABOVE A bright emerald base color had black glaze dragged over it. This toned down the brightness of the green and the contrast between the two colors has given a slightly antiqued look to this chest.

Tartan Effect

ABOVE Terra-cotta and blue stripes were dragged over an egg-yolk yellow basecoat. The stripes are the same width as the brush.

Dragging a Wall

LEFT A red terra-cotta glaze was dragged over a greenish-gray basecoat. Since the colors are close in tone, the result is even and subtle.

The Basic Technique: Flogging

FLOGGING IN CLOSE-UP

Flogging brushes have much longer bristles than dragging brushes. These produce a light stripe broken up by many small swirls. The final effect is linear, like dragging, but the stripes are broken up and more subtle. As with dragging, flogging on walls is done vertically but on wood it follows the grain.

TOOLS & MATERIALS

Flogging brush

Glaze brush

Mixed glaze

1 Apply the glaze, spreading it out thinly with the brush to form an even layer. As in dragging, paint in vertical strips to obtain uniform coverage.

2 Direct the flogging brush up and down over the glaze to emphasize the striped effect. The surface should be a little wetter than when dragging. Leave an unflogged wet edge to join the next strip.

3 Wipe off excess glaze from the brush. Starting at the bottom and using a sharp action, hit the surface with the top 2–3 in/ 50–75 mm of the brush, moving up about ¼ in/6.25 mm each time.

Flogging with Feathers

A blue glaze was thinly painted over a yellow ocher background, and hit with a bunch of feathers, starting at the base and moving upward. This gives a more random result than using a brush. Use any feathers that are long, strong, and fairly flexible – pheasant and peacock feathers, for example.

COLOR COMBINATIONS

Black on dark pink

Gray on gray-blue

Pale yellow on blue-green

Terra-cotta on primrose yellow

Flogged Stool
BELOW An olive green glaze was flogged with a brush over a pale cream basecoat to match the fabric of the seat.

Decorative Shelf
ABOVE This gothic-inspired shelf with its integral decorative bracket was flogged, using a brush, in middle-brown over a dark cream basecoat. This gives a subtle suggestion of the grain of wood without trying to imitate wood too accurately.

Patterning with Cloth

Cloth Patterned Wall and Frame

The bright yellow wall and viridian green frame were covered with orange-terracotta glaze and dark blue-green glaze respectively, and then patterned with cheesecloth/mutton cloth to give it a lightly mottled look.

THIS TECHNIQUE GIVES a cloudy, softly mottled finish. The fabric used is a fine-gauge, slightly elastic cotton knit. It is formed into a rounded pad by rolling the fabric and then tucking the ends inside the roll. The pad must be absolutely smooth since any folds in the fabric will make lines in the glaze. The delicate print of the weave is left on the glazed surface, creating a deliberately slightly uneven texture. To emphasize this, the pad can be dabbed more firmly in some areas than others. With careful application of glaze and even dabbing, the effect can be almost as regular as that made by stippling.

TOOLS & MATERIALS

Brush for applying glaze

Cheesecloth/ mutton cloth made into a pad

Mixed glaze

The Basic Technique

1 *Paint the glaze on generously. Use a strongly colored glaze to avoid patchiness, as the cheesecloth/mutton cloth will absorb the paint unevenly.*

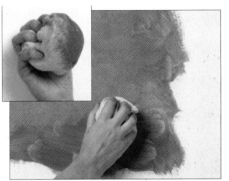

2 *Fold the cheesecloth/mutton cloth into a smooth pad. Dab it firmly over a small area. Move quickly on to the next area so the dabs overlap.*

3 *Brush more glaze into the wet edge to prepare a new area for patterning. Spread out the paint evenly and brush well into the previous area.*

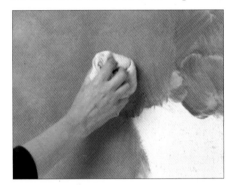

4 *Continue dabbing carefully. When the pad is saturated with glaze, turn or refold it to a clean surface to avoid reapplying glaze to the surface.*

How to Tear a Cheesecloth/Mutton Cloth

1 *To avoid using scissors, which create small threads that stick to the work, pull the end of a thread running the width of the fabric.*

2 *While holding the thread, push the gathered fabric along it until the thread either breaks or is pulled out.*

3 *The cloth can now be pulled apart and there are no raw ends to ravel.*

Patterning a Corner with Cloth

1 Paint the glaze on both walls and into the corner. Avoid letting too much glaze accumulate in the angle.

2 Fold the cloth to make a small edge that fits right into the corner without removing glaze from the other wall.

Creating a Mottled Effect

1 Brush on the glaze, covering the surface well using bold, uneven strokes.

2 Having folded the cheesecloth/ mutton cloth into a smooth pad, dab it all over the surface.

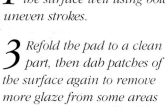

3 Refold the pad to a clean part, then dab patches of the surface again to remove more glaze from some areas than others.

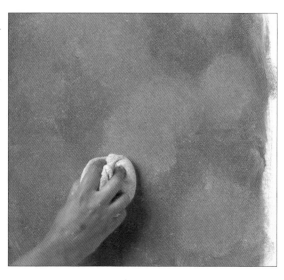

ALTERNATIVES

You can use other types of cloth to create different effects depending on the weave. A cloth with a coarser weave will produce a more textured look (below).

The sky effect (bottom) was produced by painting blue glaze unevenly over a white basecoat. After cloth patterning all over the surface, use a clean cloth to remove more glaze in patches, suggesting clouds.

Using a coarse-weave cloth

Sky effect

COLOR COMBINATIONS

*Dark blue
on dark red*

*Middle-green
on beige*

*Yellow
ocher on
terra-cotta*

*Beige on
dark blue*

Cloth Patterned Fireplace

ABOVE AND RIGHT Olive green glaze
on a brown-gray basecoat was
dabbed off with cheesecloth/
mutton cloth. A smaller piece of
cloth was used to clean areas
where too much glaze settled.

Cloth Patterned Frame

*LEFT The delicate finish on
this frame picks up the
colors in the picture. A
deep mustard ocher glaze
was applied over a dark
green basecoat and
evenly patterned.*

PITFALLS

If the glaze is dabbed off
unevenly the brushmarks will still
show in some areas. Dabbing
needs to be done systematically
and evenly. If too little pressure
is applied the same problem of
visible brushstrokes will occur.

Uneven dabbing

Rag Rolling a Corner

1 Roll the crumpled rag up the wall as near to the corner as possible but without rubbing glaze off the other wall.

2 Using a corner of the rag (or a smaller piece of cloth), dab right into the angle. Press lightly to avoid removing too much glaze.

RAG ROLLING WITH CHAMOIS LEATHER

Chamois leather, a very soft and absorbent material, leaves a strong and distinct pattern. Used wet, it creates a more definite pattern. Used dry, a chamois gives a softer, more muted look. The results of both are shown below – attractively textured surfaces resembling crushed velvet.

Using a dry chamois

Using a wet chamois

Storage Unit

ABOVE Rag rolling can be used to create a lively, contemporary look. Onto five bright, sharp base colors – orange, red, yellow, green, and blue – a clear blue glaze was stippled then rag rolled. The glaze layer successfully unites the different base colors.

Wastepaper Basket

LEFT The basket was painted a strong, deep red inside and out. Olive green glaze was stippled and rag rolled on the outside. The rich colors are particularly suited to the traditional style of the container.

Rag Rolled Wall

RIGHT The wall was painted dark green, then a pale green glaze was rag rolled in stripes, leaving a narrow strip of dark green visible in between.

Hexagonal Box

BELOW AND BELOW RIGHT The same yellow was used as the base color of both the box and its lid, uniting the two. Bright scarlet was then rag rolled on the lid and warm chocolate glazes on the box.

COLOR COMBINATIONS

Middle-green on yellow ocher

Yellow ocher on dark red

Blue-green on pale green

Terra-cotta red on beige

PITFALLS

As you roll up the walls, the cloth may slip, wiping off a patch of glaze. Avoid this by working over a small area at a time. To correct it, apply a little glaze over the bare patch, stipple it, and dab off with a cloth.

The degree of contrast between glaze color and base color is critical in rag rolling. The dark green stippling (below) is too harsh against the white base; a softer, paler glaze color would have looked better.

Smears

Tonal Contrast

Frottage

T HIS PAINT EFFECT IS achieved without glaze. Instead you apply watered-down paint over a dry painted surface and lay paper or a similar absorbent material over the wet paint, flattening it out with your hands. Some of the paint is absorbed by the paper. When the paper is removed, a random pattern of paint is left. Each new sheet of paper and fresh layer of paint produces a different effect. Although the characteristic look of frottage is achieved primarily by chance, there are ways in which it can be controlled. The absorbency of the base paint, the choice of colors and the length of time the paper is left on are all factors influencing the end result.

Frottaged Wall

Slate blue was frottaged over an olive brown basecoat. Frottage tends to produce an irregular effect, as here, with the base color showing through more clearly in some places than others.

FROTTAGE IN CLOSE-UP

Part of the unique texture produced by frottage is the small lines that are created by the "grain" of the newspaper.

TOOLS & MATERIALS

Brush for applying paint

Mixed paint

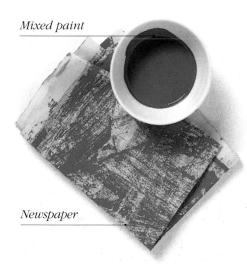

Newspaper

The Basic Technique

1 Mix the paint to the required consistency: it should be approximately two-thirds paint to one-third water. The mix may have to be adjusted according to the type of paint and the surface. Hold the newspaper up to the wall and mark the area it covers.

2 Cover the marked out area with a fairly generous amount of paint. Work quickly before it dries out.

3 Lay a sheet of newspaper over the wet painted surface. Smooth all over with the palm of your hands, taking care to apply even pressure so you will not leave hand prints.

4 Peel off the paper carefully with one hand while still holding it in place with the other.

Joining Frottage Areas

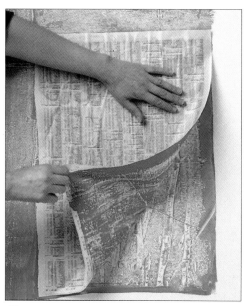

1 Move on to the next area, applying the paint up to the edge of the finished area.

2 Place the paper down on the newly painted surface and then remove it as in steps 3 and 4 of the Basic Technique.

3 There are dark lines where each new frottaged area begins. To hide these, use double frottage (see opposite).

PITFALLS

When there is too strong a color contrast between the basecoat and the topcoat, the effect is somewhat coarse (below left): for a more subtle effect choose two colors closer in tone. It is also very important that the topcoat is of the right consistency. If you dilute it with too much water the paint will become very runny, resulting in visible drips in some areas (below center). If very little water is added the effect is very dense and heavy, losing the typical texture of frottage (below right).

Colors too strong

Too much water added

Too little water added

Double Frottage

The reason why you might choose double frottage is to change the color effect and also either to emphasize or camouflage the shapes left by the paper. As you can see, this technique builds up a richly textured surface and offers endless opportunities for variations.

1 Coat a small part of your frottaged surface with diluted paint in a contrasting color. You can cover a larger area once you learn how quickly the paint dries.

2 Tear off irregularly shaped and sized pieces of newspaper and lay them over the whole of the painted area while it is still wet.

3 Smooth your hands all over the paper to ensure even contact with the paint.

4 Peel off the paper. The finished effect shows how the regular rectangles and straight lines of the first paint layer have been hidden. Lines where one patch ends are inevitable to some extent, but can be minimized by using, as here, regularly shaped pieces of paper for the first layer and irregularly shaped pieces for the second layer only.

FROTTAGE WITH OTHER MATERIALS

Crumpled tissue paper gives a smaller, more even pattern than newspaper. Here (below), blue was frottaged over a red basecoat. Finely woven cotton was used to frottage the warm orange-brown and green, and blue stripes over the pale orange basecoat (right).

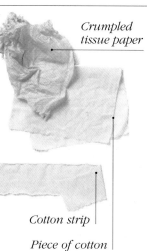

Crumpled tissue paper

Cotton strip

Piece of cotton

Frottage with tissue paper

Frottage with fabric and three colors

Double Frottage

ABOVE Reddish brown paint was frottaged over a grayish brown basecoat. To soften the effect yellow ocher was frottaged over this.

Hanging Box

ABOVE The warm yellow ocher basecoat and rich terra-cotta topcoat complement each other well on this box. Pieces of paper were torn to the correct width in order to frottage inside the compartments.

COLOR COMBINATIONS

Dark blue on bright red

Frottaged Desk

LEFT AND BELOW *Rich dark green was painted and then frottaged over a deep red basecoat. The dark colors suit the classic shape of the desk and give a convincingly antique effect, as shown in the close-up.*

Off-white on light blue

Dark green on turquoise blue

Frottaging a Chair

LEFT AND ABOVE *The chair was painted a strong, bright orange and then frottaged over with a cooler blue paint. The bold, strongly contrasting colors give the chair a lively modern look, showing how versatile this technique can be.*

Dark red on blue-green

Woodgraining

Woodgrained Chair

A simple, 1930s-style chair was given a maple-effect grain by using a warm, ginger-colored glaze over a yellow ocher basecoat. The baseboard was grained to match. The close-up detail shows how a darker glaze on the center panel gives a more pronounced grain.

USING PAINT TO IMITATE wood is a very old craft. It has probably been practiced for 200 years using the same techniques as today. Although wood can seem intimidating, it is not really a difficult technique. The wood effects shown here, mahogany, oak, and maple, exemplify a range of basic techniques and illustrate the use of essential tools. Once the basics are mastered, these skills can be adapted to reproduce numerous other woods. Achieving a convincing finish can seem quite daunting, but accurate color makes an enormous difference to the result and so careful study of real wood will pay off. Using the correct tools will also help, but you may prefer to try out some of the techniques with adapted tools and brushes before investing.

TOOLS & MATERIALS

Glaze

Flat brush for applying glaze and graining maple

Flogging brushes of different widths for oak and mahogany

Cork cut to wedge shape

Cotton rag to cover cork for oak graining

Fine cotton or open-weave cloth

Steel combs with different teeth sizes

Badger-hair softening brush

Mottler for mahogany

Mahogany Graining

Mahogany graining is best used on surfaces that are large enough to show the characteristic arch-shaped heart or "flame" to its best advantage. The sample below shows a warm, deep red mahogany, an effect which is recreated by painting dark chocolate brown glaze over a dark reddish-pink basecoat.

1 *Paint on the glaze vertically with a flat brush. Spread it out so the basecoat is visible (inset). Using a dry flogging brush, tap the bristles at 1 in/25 mm intervals, working up from the bottom.*

2 *Dry off the flat brush. Create a half arch shape by moving the sides of the bristles in a wavy diagonal. Move up in successive arches, varying the pressure (but not too regularly) to resemble light and dark grain.*

3 *To vary the shapes you make, twist the brush so that the bristles are at right-angles to the surface.*

4 *Pull the mottler down in some areas, following the arch shape. Vary pressure to make darker and lighter marks, imitating mahogany's undulating grain.*

Oak Graining

To show off the beauty of oak graining you need a fairly large area, such as a door. The finish is easier to achieve on a flat or only slightly curved surface. Oak graining can look cool and delicate when you use creams and grays, or warm when rich or dark brown glazes are chosen. For the middle-brown color shown below, use burnt umber glaze over a cream basecoat.

1 *Work in panels about 18in/45cm wide and 1 or 2 yards/1–2 meters high – like planks of real wood – according to the area being covered. Apply the glaze vertically with a flat brush.*

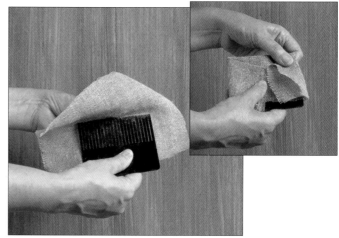

2 *Fold a piece of fine cotton or open-weave cloth around a wide-toothed metal comb, tucking the edges in so that it is easy to handle.*

3 *Pull the covered comb downward in a vertical line, twisting it very slightly to left and right to achieve the wavy look of real wood.*

4 *While the glaze is still wet, go over the surface with a finer-toothed comb. Work at a slight diagonal to break up the vertical lines and make the light "dashes" typical of oak grain.*

Graining with a Cork

1 *You can imitate the small half-arch shapes that appear on oak by using a cork. Sharpen a cork to a wedge shape and wrap it in a cloth.*

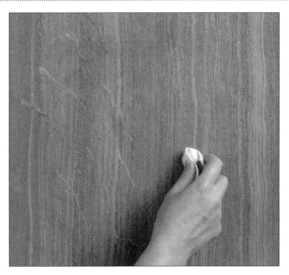

2 *Draw small half-arch shapes, making them look random by pressing harder at first, then relaxing the pressure. Group them together in areas and leave other patches free. Study real oak to see where these marks occur so you can reproduce them convincingly.*

Maple Graining

This is a soft, delicate effect, particularly good on small items such as frames, boxes, and lamp bases. Below, a light, warm brown glaze is used over a honey-colored basecoat. For a richer look, a yellow ocher basecoat could be used, or a pink-toned basecoat with a chocolate brown glaze. This technique can be adapted to achieve a satinwood or rosewood effect.

1 *Apply the glaze in one direction with a flat brush, spreading it out so the basecoat shows through.*

2 *While the glaze is still wet, gently twist a mottler from side to side while moving it over the surface. Press on the bristles when changing direction to release more glaze, giving spots of color typical of maple.*

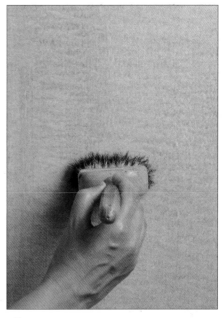

3 *Before the glaze is dry, brush over the surface with a softening brush to blend in the darker areas. Do not make the color too uniform. You can omit this stage if you like the effect already achieved.*

Woodgraining Alternatives

The details show oak graining (right) on pale gray, with darker gray glaze; bird's-eye maple (below) in rich, warm colors with minimum contrast between tones; and walnut graining (below right) in paler, colder colors, here, cool brown on greenish-yellow ocher.

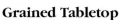

Oak graining (above)

Maple graining (above)

Walnut graining (right)

Grained Tabletop

RIGHT *This elegant tabletop shows maple graining used to simulate different wood veneers. Different shades of brown glaze were used and it was softened on the paler areas to recreate the look of satinwood. The black banding and stenciled motif imitate ebony effectively.*

Tall Shelf Unit

ABOVE *This unit is made from old, rough wood. Its rustic look was emphasized by the deliberately strong contrast between the reddish-pink basecoat and the brown glaze, which was deepened with a little dark blue.*

Decorative Wooden Case

BELOW The main panel was grained to imitate burr walnut with dark brown glaze over an orange basecoat. The central motif was stenciled on and glaze was dabbed on and blended, using a softening brush, to resemble satinwood. The outer band was initially treated using the mahogany technique and adapted to imitate rosewood.

Coal Bucket

ABOVE This old metal coal bucket has a new lease on life as a decorative object with an oak-grain treatment, a typical Victorian effect. At that time metal was beginning to replace wood for many domestic items, but since it was an unfamiliar material, it was often disguised to look like wood.

PITFALLS

Important tips for achieving convincing wood finishes are to judge the colors carefully and to mix a translucent glaze that will not mask the base color. In the example (below left), too little glaze has been used over the basecoat, so the effect is dull and opaque. The detail (below center) shows the crude result when the glaze color and basecoat contrast too sharply. The example (below right) shows how unrealistic graining looks when the brushmarks are painted too evenly.

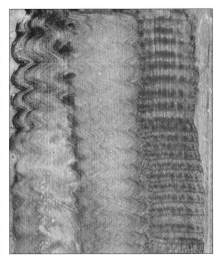

Not enough glaze

Wrong basecoat color

Brushmarks too regular

Decorative Graining

**Decoratively
Grained Wall**

*This boldly colored modern
room uses almost comple-
mentary shades of scarlet
and blue to dramatic
effect. Gray-blue glaze was
grained with the "oak" edge
of the roller (see p. 77).*

WITH WOODGRAINING the intention is to imitate natural wood as
closely as possible. However, you can also achieve a colorful and
decorative effect with different types of flexible combs and
rollers. The purpose is not to create a totally convincing replica, but to produce the look of painted oak and pine quickly and easily. The same method
can be used to simulate moiré silk or other fabrics. You can experiment with
overlaying patterns and colors, remembering that this technique is more
suited to bold than subtle effects.

TOOLS & MATERIALS

The Basic Technique

Plastic graining roller with removable head for wide or thin grains

Soft plastic graining combs with two different widths

Glaze

Cloth to wipe off excess glaze from comb and surface

Flogging brush for softening

Brush for applying glaze

1 Apply the glaze vertically, and brush it out to give a thin translucent covering. Wipe over with a soft cloth so that only a very thin layer of glaze is left.

2 Apply the top of the roller to the glazed surface. Rock the roller halfway down its length to achieve the grained effect, the top of the head gives the broad effect of oak grain.

3 Work down the wall from the top, rocking the roller very slightly at intervals. You may want to use both hands to ensure firm contact with the surface.

4 Remove excess glaze built up at the top of the head with a soft cloth (inset). You can achieve the narrower effect of pine grain by rocking the roller all the way down and then up again. This produces characteristic circular knot shapes. Space these irregularly.

Softening the Pattern

The grained effect can be left as previously shown, but if you want to heighten the look of moiré silk rather than wood, or simply to make the effect less strong, the finish can be softened with a flogging, dragging, or softening brush. A flogging brush, as used below, emphasizes the fabric effect. This is enhanced even more if a soft color similar to the glaze is used for the base.

Using the flogging brush, lightly pull down the bristles over the thin and still slightly wet glaze. This will blur the edges of the "knots."

To accentuate the look of fabric and soften the effect even more, the flogging brush can be brushed across horizontally as well as vertically.

Different Types of Grain

These pictures (right) show the different surfaces of the graining roller heads and the oak and pine effects they can create.

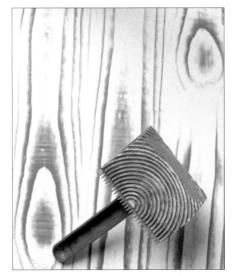

Oak effect

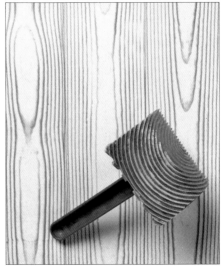

Pine effect

COLOR COMBINATIONS

Brown on beige

Light blue on dark blue

Strong green on clear yellow

Strong pink on bright pink

Bedside Cabinet

LEFT *This small cabinet was painted dark blue and a grayish white glaze was applied over it. The graining comb was used just to make a swirling pattern rather than to imitate wood.*

Picture Frame

ABOVE *Green glaze was painted over a reddish-brown basecoat. Since the comb was wider than the frame, only the middle section of the roller was used. The result is a woodgrained look, but in deliberately unnatural colors.*

PITFALLS

If the glaze is too thick and wet, the graining looks heavy. Here, the color also contrasts too strongly with the white background and the graining is too regular for it to have a natural look. Avoid repeating the rocking motion too often, since it creates unattractive breaks and lines across the grain.

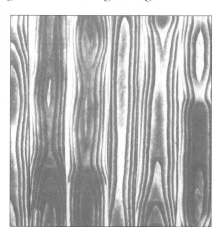

Too heavily lined

Broken grain

Marbling

Marbled Chest

The panels of this chest were marbled using a soft, warm raw sienna deepened with a little raw umber. After the initial layer of glaze was applied, the panels were sponged, ragged, and veined. The surrounds were painted a deep green-blue.

MARBLING, LIKE WOODGRAINING, is a technique in which one material is painted to imitate another. To achieve a convincing result it is important to study examples of real marble. But because real marble comes in so many different colors and patterns, you can work more freely than when woodgraining. Marbling techniques are very flexible. The first step is the subtle blending of softened tones but then other methods, such as sponging, splattering, or veining with artist's brushes or a feather, can be used separately or together. Marbling is traditionally done on structural surfaces, such as walls, floors, and pillars but it can be just as effective on small items, such as lamp bases, boxes, and frames. The finished work should be sealed with gloss or semigloss varnish both to protect the surface and give it the shiny look of real marble.

TOOLS & MATERIALS

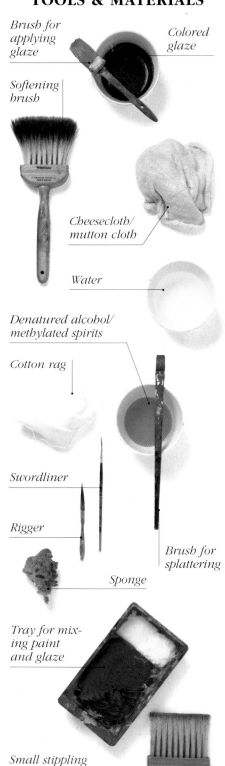

Brush for applying glaze

Colored glaze

Softening brush

Cheesecloth/ mutton cloth

Water

Denatured alcohol/ methylated spirits

Cotton rag

Swordliner

Rigger

Brush for splattering

Sponge

Tray for mixing paint and glaze

Small stippling brush for use on moldings

The Basic Technique

1 Color the glaze, ensuring that it remains transparent. Mix only a little at a time, this way the shade of each batch will vary. Apply the glaze diagonally, varying the angle and thickness of the brushstrokes.

2 Add darker paint to the glaze and apply it in patches, strengthening some of the existing darker areas. Aim to establish three tones: light, medium, and dark.

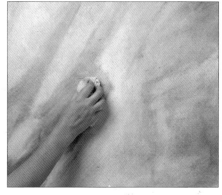

3 Fold cheesecloth/mutton cloth into a smooth pad and dab the glaze in the lighter areas to remove brushstrokes and even out the colors.

4 Now dab the darker areas. Treating dark and light areas separately keeps them well defined and contrasting.

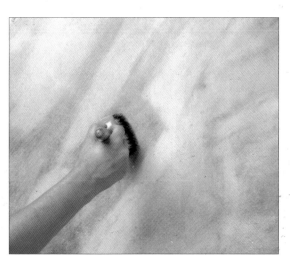

5 While the glaze is still wet, use the softening brush to remove the cheesecloth/ mutton cloth marks. If you let the glaze dry out you will be unable to remove them. Hold the brush at right angles to the surface and move it from side to side, using your arm, not your wrist, to achieve a smooth effect without creating visible brushstrokes. You can then add veins, if desired (see p. 82).

Veining

It is not essential to add veins to make marbling look realistic, but although tricky to do well, veining can look very effective. Always work around the shapes and colors of the basic marbling, emphasizing and outlining the darker shapes. Veining is done with slightly thinned paint, not glaze, and in a color just a little darker than the base shade. Various tools can be used for veining, including artist's brushes, feathers, and a special brush used just for painting lines called a swordliner. You can use a rigger, a short smaller brush that makes thinner lines, to reduce veins that are too thick.

Using Artist's Brushes

1 Use a small artist's fitch, made of soft bristle, to outline darker areas or create veins of varying thickness. Do not hold the brush like a pencil, but allow it to move loosely so that the veins do not look too tightly drawn.

2 Go over the veins with a softening brush so that they gently blend into the background. Use the brush as in The Basic Technique, step 5 (see p. 81).

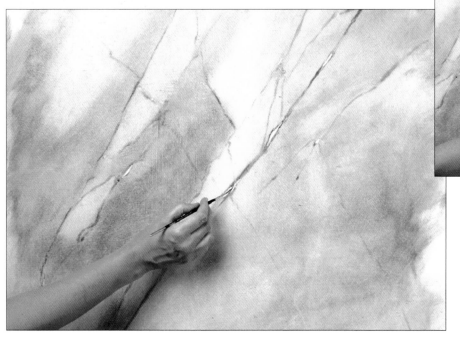

3 Lighten thick areas by dipping a rigger in water and removing a little paint to reveal the white base and form a lighter "island" within a vein (left). This can only be done while the paint is still wet. To soften the effect further, rag the veins gently with a cotton cloth to break up the veining slightly (above).

Using a Swordliner

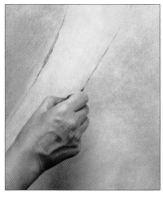

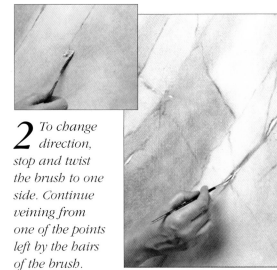

1 *Use the tip of the brush to start the vein, then increase the pressure to broaden the line.*

2 *To change direction, stop and twist the brush to one side. Continue veining from one of the points left by the hairs of the brush.*

3 *You can add to the veining with a rigger, complementing the shapes made by the swordliner. It is used in the same way – by stopping the line and twisting the brush.*

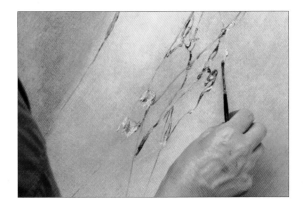

Using a Feather

Any long, strong feathers – such as goose, duck, or peacock – are suitable for veining. Use a feather with the longer barbs on the right for veins starting at the top left, and vice versa. Dip the feather in the paint, dab it on to the surface, then drag across it. Since the feather is curved, this may feel awkward at first, but this method produces authentically irregular veins.

PITFALLS

If you drag the side rather than the tip of the softening brush along the surface you will get scratches (below).

Veining can look crude and artificial for several reasons. Here (bottom), the lines are too dark and positioned arbitrarily, without relating to the dark and light areas in the basecoat. The three lines at the top right are too evenly spaced and the wiggly line looks unnatural. The thickness of the lines is too regular. Veins should start at the side of the work and vary from thick to thin, eventually petering out altogether. Take care not to cross lines, as shown. The meeting point of veins should either form a little "island" or the line should continue on the other side a small distance away from the meeting point.

Scratches

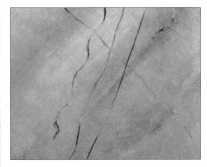

Artificial looking lines

Splatter Marbling

Some natural marbles have a pattern of small spots and few or no veins. Marbling to achieve this kind of effect is useful for small objects where an intense overall look is required. Splatter marbling is a technique that can be used on both horizontal and vertical surfaces and it can be used to cover a whole area or just part of a larger marbled surface to give a bit of variety.

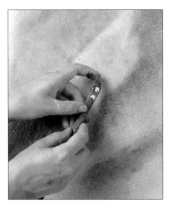

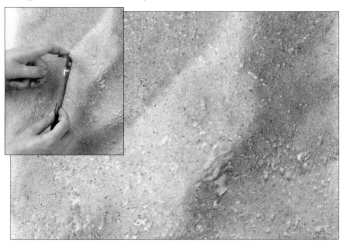

1 While the basecoat is still wet, take a small stiff brush, dip it in water, and using your finger, splatter the water over the surface.

2 Go over the area immediately with a softening brush to reveal the spots made by the water. Do this lightly or the spots will be smoothed out.

3 For greater depth and variety mix a little darker paint with the water and splatter small areas. Soften gently. The final result is a mixture of light and dark spots of varying sizes.

Marbling a Cornice

1 Apply thin, clear, or light-colored glaze to the surface, taking care not to let glaze build up in the crevices. Paint on veins in a diagonal direction, varying the thickness of the lines. Apply the paint quite thinly so that the veins do not look heavy.

2 Dab over the veins with a stippling brush along the direction of the line. Wipe the bristles on a cloth from time to time to remove excess paint and glaze. Repeat as necessary until the vein looks soft.

Marbling Panels

1 Real marble comes in slabs. For an authentic look on a wall divide it into suitably sized panels, marking the edges with a soft pencil.

2 Marble a panel, then wipe off any glaze that has spread over the pencil line into the next panel.

3 Marble every other panel and allow it to dry completely, preferably overnight. Then marble the unpainted panels in the same way.

4 Wipe off any glaze that has gone onto the adjacent panel. The pencil line should show through and resemble the gap between slabs. It can be deepened with a darker pencil if desired.

5 To harmonize the panels, you can add in some more veins at this stage, or veins can be darkened, as shown here, to match veining elsewhere.

Floating Marble

Floating marble is a quick and effective technique that you can use on horizontal surfaces, such as tabletops and floors. Here, strong, bright colors are used, but the technique also works particularly well with very dark, more subtle shades such as the greens used on the plaque opposite. You can also do this technique using one color only to give an overall textured effect.

1 Apply one colored glaze in patches, spreading it out well over the surface.

2 Paint the second color on the bare areas. With a smooth pad of folded cheesecloth/mutton cloth dab over first one color, then the other, using a clean part of the pad to avoid mixing and muddying the colors.

3 Go over the whole surface gently with a softening brush to even out the glaze.

4 Dip the softening brush in water and dab it all over the surface, forming small spots.

5 Next dip the softening brush in denatured alcohol/methylated spirits and dab it over the surface. The combination of glaze, water, and denatured alcohol/methylated spirits will produce spots and blotches of different sizes. Allow the surface to dry without softening it.

Picture Frame

LEFT The floating technique was used here, with water, denatured alcohol/methylated spirits, and paint used alternately to build up layers of spots and patches. The off-white veins were painted on diagonally as if the whole frame were one piece of marble.

Floating Marbling on a Panel

RIGHT Over a white basecoat, blue and terra-cotta glazes created this floating marble surface. This can be used on floors or any other flat surface.

Marbled Plaque

RIGHT AND BELOW This plaster plaque was painted black and then glazed with several shades of dark green, using the floating method to reveal the layers and create spots of different colors.

Sponge Marbling

This technique is particularly suitable for small areas and objects. A sponge is dipped in water and then dabbed over the surface to lift off glaze, leaving lighter spots and blobs. Then darker paint is dabbed on for contrast. Experiment with doing more or less of the two stages to achieve a result you like.

Choose a sponge with large holes so the paint leaves a more positive mark.

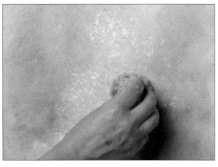

1 Apply the glaze so that there are dark and light areas. While the surface is still wet, dab over the lighter areas with a damp sponge.

2 Thin paint in a slightly darker shade than the glaze color so that it flows freely. Dip a clean sponge in the paint, using a tray so that the sponge can be squeezed out slightly so it is not too saturated. Dab the sponge on the darker areas, lightly at first to judge the effect. More layers can be built up for a more strongly contrasting look.

Candlestick

RIGHT The effect here is of granite, achieved by the sponge method with first gray, then black glaze applied over an off-white basecoat.

Marbled Case

ABOVE AND RIGHT The border was painted to imitate dramatic black and sienna Porto d'Oro marble. The inner panel has a white basecoat painted over with very faint black veins to resemble Carrara marble, then stippled over slightly for a trompe-l'œil look.

Marbled Door

LEFT Over a white basecoat,
raw sienna, raw umber, and
white were sponge marbled
around the edge of this door,
and splatter marbled on the
inside panel. The effect is
light and warm.

COLOR COMBINATIONS

*Deep blue-green
with white veins
on gray*

*Beige with
dark cool
brown veins
on white*

Cool Gray Mirror

ABOVE This mirror was painted white and
splatter marbled with different proportions
of ultra-marine blue, raw umber and white,
giving a gray-blue looking, cold marble effect.

*Black veins
on trans-
parent glaze*

Splatter Marbled Candlestick

LEFT A wooden candlestick was painted light,
cool brown. The splatter technique was then
applied using various proportions of raw
umber and white. When this coat was dry
a second layer using burnt sienna was
randomly applied in the same way. The two
layers of dark colors give the candlestick
a solid, heavy look.

*White and
terra-cotta
on black*

Stencil Effects

The art of stenciling is very ancient and has been used by many cultures in different periods as a form of decoration. This chapter demonstrates a variety of techniques that you can use to create beautiful patterns on many items in your home.

Tools and Materials

A LL THE STENCILING techniques call for three main types of equipment: materials to design and cut stencils (below); materials for attaching and marking out stencils (right); and materials for printing stencil designs (below right). Concentrate first on learning how to apply paint using brushes – to start, a medium-size brush is probably best – a small roller, and some sponges to experiment with.

Designing and Cutting Stencils

BELOW AND RIGHT Stencils are cut from poster board, also known as stencil card, or acetate using a craft knife or heat knife. When using a craft knife, cut on a cutting board that leaves no score marks that might interfere with subsequent cutting. When using a heat knife (see p. 98) – the quickest and easiest tool for cutting acetate stencils – cut on a piece of glass.

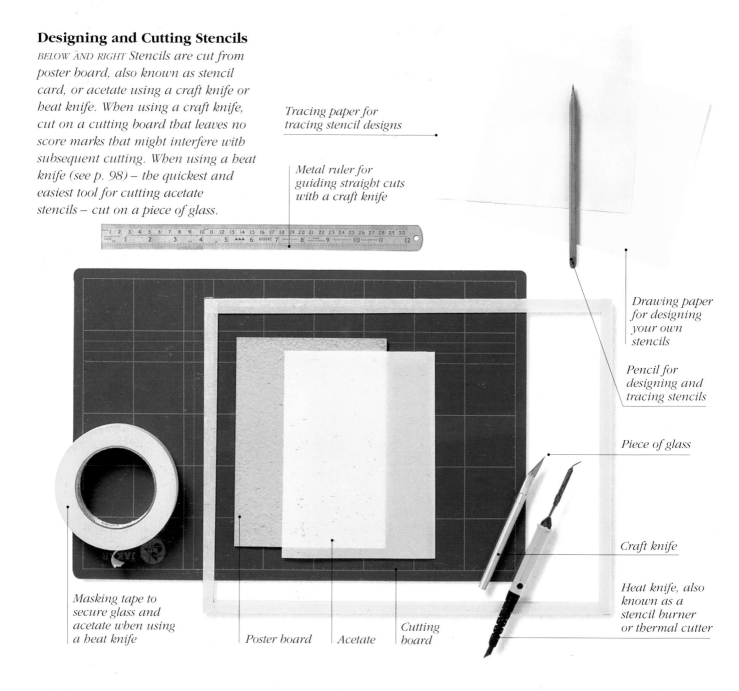

Tracing paper for tracing stencil designs

Metal ruler for guiding straight cuts with a craft knife

Drawing paper for designing your own stencils

Pencil for designing and tracing stencils

Piece of glass

Craft knife

Heat knife, also known as a stencil burner or thermal cutter

Masking tape to secure glass and acetate when using a heat knife

Poster board

Acetate

Cutting board

Positioning and Attaching Stencils

BELOW AND RIGHT To make sure your design is aligned, mark out your stencil positions, especially on large surfaces, before applying paint. You can make a simple chalk line on a wall by wiping a piece of string with children's chalk, but the chalk line shown here is more efficient. Create a simple plumb line with string and mounting putty/Blu-Tack. Use masking tape (see p. 92) or repositioning glue/Spray Mount to attach the stencil to the surface and newspaper to mask areas you don't want stenciled. The fumes of the spray can be hazardous, so wear a face mask and work in a well-ventilated area.

Newspaper

Repositioning glue/Spray Mount

String

Chalk line

Mounting putty/Blu-Tack

Applying Paint

BELOW AND RIGHT Apply paint to your stencils using brushes, rollers, and sponges. Large rollers are best for painting wall stencils, especially if you are using only one color. For brush stenciling, you can start off with only one or two brushes, but you may need more as your stencils become more intricate and colorful.

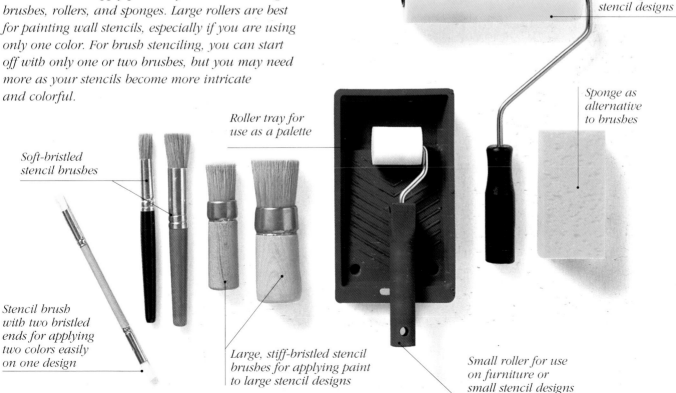

Large roller for use on walls and large stencil designs

Sponge as alternative to brushes

Roller tray for use as a palette

Soft-bristled stencil brushes

Stencil brush with two bristled ends for applying two colors easily on one design

Large, stiff-bristled stencil brushes for applying paint to large stencil designs

Small roller for use on furniture or small stencil designs

Paints

ALTHOUGH SPECIFIC PAINTS are made for stenciling and stamping, you can in fact use any paint. The particular paint you choose depends on your own preferences and the type of tools you use to paint your stencil. Generally, you should avoid paints that are too diluted since they may seep under the stencil; but if you want to use a roller, you will need a paint that is sufficiently liquid, yet opaque, so that you can roll the roller through it. An intricate stencil may work best with spray paint, while for specialized projects oil-base or watercolor paints, waxes or special fabric paints may be desirable. The trick with any paint, however, is to use it sparingly. A small amount goes a long way.

Water-base Paints

ABOVE AND RIGHT *Water-base paints, also known as acrylic paints, dry quickly, allowing you to add to both the stencil and the surface without fear of smudging. You can also wash the tools in water after use. Artist's acrylic paint is solid and best used only for brush stenciling. Decorator's paint is made especially for stenciling and stamping. Household paint, such as vinyl or latex/ emulsion, tends to be too liquid to use.*

Decorator's paint

Artist's acrylic paint

Artist's oil paint

Oil-base paint

Oil-base Paints

ABOVE *Oil-base paints – especially artist's paints, which come in many colors – work well for stenciling. But they dry slowly, so overlapping stencil designs may cause some smudging. Oil-base paints are not recommended for stamping.*

Spray paint

Spray Paints

ABOVE AND RIGHT *Spray paints are useful for stenciling on various surfaces, including glass and fabric. You can even use spray paints intended for cars. Breathing the fumes of spray paints is hazardous, so wear a face mask and work in a well-ventilated area.*

Gold-colored metallic wax

Metallic Waxes

ABOVE AND RIGHT *Metallic waxes are useful for brush stenciling. They are particularly helpful to beginners because the wax is dry and therefore does not run or smudge.*

Metallic wax stick

Artist's watercolor paint

Watercolor Paints

ABOVE *Watercolor paints cannot be used for stamping or stenciling, because they are too thin. But they are ideal for hand painting over a solid stenciled base.*

Fabric paints

Fabric Paints

ABOVE *Fabric paints are effective and washable for both stenciling and stamping. You can use ordinary paints instead, but the color will wash out, leaving only a faint pattern.*

Cutting Ready-designed Stencils

Stencil Examples

A poster board stencil is heavier than an acetate stencil but is more rigid, making it easier to handle and so more suitable for large designs. An acetate stencil can be more difficult to handle but is easier to cut and suitable for small, intricate designs.

Y OU CAN BUY READY-DESIGNED stencils from art supply and decorating stores. Some of these are precut. Others come on poster board or acetate and need to be cut out. Still others consist of a design you need to transfer to poster board or acetate and then cut out. Both poster board and acetate can be cut with a strong, sharp, craft knife. While poster board is inexpensive, many people find that cutting it with a craft knife is hard work. For an easier and quicker method that does not rely so much on hand pressure, you may want to stick to acetate. Keep in mind that acetate is more difficult to handle than poster board, particularly when producing very large designs, because it can bend and curl easily.

A poster board stencil suitable for brush or roller stenciling (see pp. 100–109)

Two acetate stencils most suitable for brush stenciling (see pp. 100–105)

Delicate designs cut in acetate, suitable for spray stenciling (see pp. 110–115)

Acetate stencil made of both positive and negative designs

A positive and a reverse stencil cut from poster board

Acetate stencils for the stained glass effect (see p. 104)

A large design in acetate suitable for roller stenciling (see pp 106–109)

Cutting a Poster Board Stencil

1 Preprinted stencils from books are normally printed on poster board. To make the poster board paint-proof, dab the entire surface with a mixture of 1 part boiled lin-seed oil to 1 part turpentine. Leave to dry for 10 minutes.

2 Cut out the design, using a sharp craft knife. Hold the knife like a pencil and cut on a hard-surfaced cutting board such as the one shown. Cutting on wood or poster board may cause score lines that affect the stencil cutting.

3 To cut a curve, turn the poster board while keeping the craft knife in one place (right). This helps create a line that is smooth, rather than jagged or angular.

Tracing a Stencil

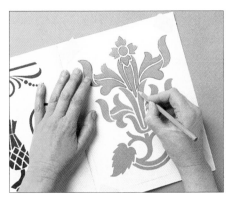

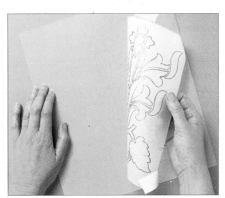

1 Fix a piece of tracing paper or waxed paper (which is less transparent) over the design with masking tape, and trace the design with a soft pencil (2B is ideal).

2 Turn the tracing paper over and tape it to a sheet of paint-proof poster board, leaving a border of 1–2in/2.5–5cm around the design. Trace over your pencil lines.

3 Check the imprint left by your pencil before removing the tracing paper. The poster board is now ready for cutting, as shown above.

Using Stencil Brushes

Brush-stenciled Table

This simple table has been given a country treatment. Old-fashioned, muted colors were applied over its original worn brown basecoat, using the stippled, swirled, and wiped techniques (see p. 101) to highlight the texture of the fruit and foliage.

Brushes work especially well for creating both traditional country designs, which use a painterly style, and formal Victorian designs, in which each part of the design is done in a different color. You can use the brush to stipple – lightly dab the surface with the tip of the brush – to create a dotted effect, swirl it in all directions for a soft effect, or wipe from side to side to create a striped effect. By wiping the brush from the tip to the base of a leaf shape, you can use the brushstroke to define the leaf. Carrying small amounts of color from one part of a design to another will add unity to your design. For example, if you are using green on a leaf, add a little green to the edges of the flower, and vice versa. As with all forms of stenciling, the trick is to use very little, dry paint (see p. 94).

TOOLS & MATERIALS

Roller tray used as a palette

Medium-size stencil brushes

Sponge, an alternative to brushes

Acetate stencils

Paper towel for removing excess paint

Masking tape

Repositioning glue/Spray Mount

The Basic Technique

1 To get a striped effect on this leaf (above), pull the brush from tip to stem in a wiping motion (right).

2 To create a softer effect than the stripes created by the wiped technique, swirl the brush around in several directions, as on the pumpkin.

4 You can also combine the three different techniques – wiping, swirling, and stippling – on parts of the design. To give the design coherence, one color should overlap onto several areas.

3 When combining several colors, as on the pear (inset), use the brush to stipple, lightly pushing the bristles vertically onto the surface to create small dots of color.

Using Metallic Wax

You can use metallic wax (see p. 95) to imitate bronze powder work. After stenciling, allow the wax to dry overnight, then protect it with a coat of shellac followed by a coat of oil-base varnish. For the best effect use wax against a dark, rich background or on off-white.

1 Dip the brush into some metallic wax. Wipe the excess on a paper towel. Apply the wax in a swirling motion (above and right).

2 To give a three-dimensional feel, add more metallic wax in a different shade. Here, a dark and a light gold metallic wax were used together.

Brush Stenciling on Fabric

Special paints are available for use on fabric. These usually need to be ironed afterward, to set the paint, making it wash resistant. If the fabric will not need washing, you can use ordinary water-base paint instead. Washing will not completely remove this paint, but will leave a soft effect.

1 Put absorbent paper under the fabric – the paint will seep through – and tape down the fabric to keep it flat. Fix the stencil in place. Apply a small amount of paint in a swirling motion.

2 Apply a second color in selected places with the same technique. This will give the design a three-dimensional quality. Be careful not to apply too much paint, as a little goes a long way.

3 Before you move on to another part of the surface, check to see how the fabric is receiving the paint. Some fabrics are more absorbent than others.

4 Here, the design was carried through in a half-drop repeat. The slight variation in color each time the stencil is applied is all part of the hand-painted look.

Using a Sponge

You can also use a small sponge to apply paint, adding different colors to a single design, just as with a stencil brush. The finished effect depends on the type of sponge you use – ranging from the fine or coarse texture of a synthetic sponge to the random texture of a natural sponge.

1 *Dab your sponge into paint (see p. 94) the consistency of light/single cream – neither too pastelike nor too watery. Apply it lightly to the stencil, using a stippling motion.*

2 *Rinse the sponge. When dry, apply a second color. Use a sponge that is just large enough to touch more than one cutout at a time, to create a mix of colors.*

3 *The end result shows the texture of the sponge. The touches of pink on the green leaves give them a lively, three-dimensional look (right).*

PITFALLS

If you apply paint too thickly, using either a brush or a sponge, the effect is very solid and rather childish (near right). Test for excess paint on a piece of scrap paper. If you use too many colors at once and work them for too long, the result is muddy and heavy (far right).

Paint too thick

Too many colors

Stained Glass Effect

This effect is best achieved with a brush or sponge that is small enough to allow you to isolate a single area of the design and paint it individually. The stencil consists of thin lines, like the lead divisions in a stained glass window, and the result, especially if stenciled against a dark color, resembles stained glass work.

1 *Fix the stencil in place with repositioning glue/Spray Mount. Apply the first color to one area of your stencil – here, the flower – using the swirling technique. To prevent a buildup of paint along the bridges, apply paint mainly in the middle of each shape.*

2 *Apply a second color to the next area of your stencil – here, the background – using the swirling technique. Again, apply paint mainly in the center of each shape. As in stained glass work, the two colors should not blend into each other.*

3 *Use a slightly damp cloth to remove a little paint from the middle of each shape (above), leaving more paint at the edges. This gives the appearance of light coming through the stencil (right).*

Stippled and Wiped Chair

ABOVE *Three stencils were used on this chair – two flowers on the three back slats, and a border of leaves on the legs and front. Orange, pale yellow, and bright blue were applied in various combinations, using both the stippled and wiped techniques.*

Small Stippled Bowl

ABOVE *This wooden bowl was frottaged (see p. 65) in blue over terra-cotta. A simple design was then stenciled around the edges of the bowl, using the stippled and wiped methods.*

Soldier Cushion

RIGHT Two stencils were used on this plain blue cushion cover. The tree was printed in dark blue, then overprinted with white leaves. Strong, contrasting colors added dynamic accents to the soldier. The soldier's feet were used as a border in dark yellow.

Fruit Tray

LEFT The wiped brush technique predominates on this stencil. The mix of colors gives the fruit a lively, three-dimensional look.

Fleur-de-lis Table

ABOVE AND BELOW A bit of the wood showing through the blue-gray basecoat of this table adds interest to the leaves and fleurs-de-lis stenciled in gray, green, blue, and deep red.

COLOR COMBINATIONS

Olive-greens and ochers on deep terra-cotta

Blues and reds on off-white

Slightly muted clear colors on warm yellow

Metallic waxes on deep blue

Using Rollers

A ROLLER PROVIDES A quick way to stencil, especially over large areas such as walls and floors. It gives the stencil either a flat, solid look or a slightly speckled appearance, depending on how much paint and pressure you apply. Even with a traditional design, a roller tends to give the finished stencil a modern look. Stencils designed for use with a roller generally have larger holes, because the roller may miss parts of too small and intricate a design. It is easy to do a stencil in one color but by carefully manipulating the roller, it is also possible to apply several colors at one time, using either the same roller or several different ones. The smaller the roller, the more manageable it will be.

Roller-stenciled Chest of Drawers

This design used olive-green, yellow ocher, and terra-cotta, randomly stenciled with a roller over the blue base on this small chest of drawers. The close-up detail shows how the texture was varied by rolling over parts of the leaves with the edge of the roller, making lines and thicker patches of paint in some areas.

TOOLS & MATERIALS

Acetate stencil

*Roller tray
and roller*

Paint

*Paper for
removing
excess paint*

Masking tape

*Repositioning
glue/Spray Mount*

The Basic Technique

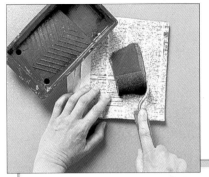

1 Load the roller with a little paint (see
p. 94). If paint oozes from the sponge
when you apply pressure to the roller on
paper, you have too much paint. Remove
the excess by rolling it on paper (left).

2 Fix the stencil in place (see p. 93).
Apply the roller in an irregular
pattern over areas of the design (below).

3 Apply a contrasting
second color, in some
places over the first color and
in other places on its own.
Most areas of the stencil
should contain both colors to
give it a three-dimensional,
unified effect.

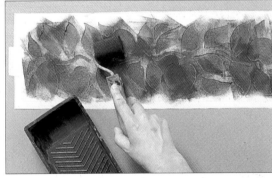

4 Partly remove the
stencil (right) to check
that the paint has gone on
as required. Here, the roller
was used to define the two
sides of the leaves (inset).

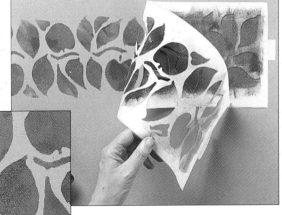

Varying Paint Thickness

1 Fix the stencil (see p. 93) and roll lightly over it with the sponge roller and paint.

2 You can apply the paint thinly, using a roller containing a little, nearly dry, paint. This creates a light, speckled effect that lets your base color show through.

3 To create an even, opaque effect either apply two thin coats of paint or apply one thick coat using a roller saturated with paint or apply more pressure to the roller.

Using Two Colors

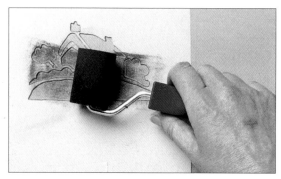

1 Put two colors in the tray, one on each side. Roll the sponge so that it picks up both colors.

2 Apply the roller to your stencil. Do not roll in too many directions, or the separate colors will merge together and become muddy.

ALTERNATIVE

After you have completed your stencil (either with a single color; two colors applied separately, as in *The Basic Technique* [see p. 107]; or two colors applied at the same time, as in *Using Two Colors* [left]), you can repeat the process by moving the stencil slightly. This allows you to apply an additional color deliberately off-register. The first coat should be fairly solid, with lighter pressure used for the topcoat. Carefully done, this technique creates an unusual highlight for a design.

3 Here, terra-cotta on the right of the roller has colored the main section of the house, while olive green on the left of the roller has colored the ground. The left of the roller was also used to paint olive green on the roof.

Stenciled Box

LEFT AND ABOVE A repeating design was stenciled in a dark neutral color onto the frottaged box (see p. 65). The stencil appears solid and even, in contrast to the bright textured background.

COLOR COMBINATIONS

Green-gray on blue

Brown on beige

Pale ocher on dark red

Blue and White Wall

ABOVE A roller was used lightly on most of this design – based on old Chinese wallpaper – to give a stippled effect. Below the chair rail, a roller was used with more pressure to create a stronger effect.

Blue-black on wood

PITFALLS

To prevent paint from seeping under your stencil (right), make sure the roller is not too wet (particularly after washing it) or overloaded with paint. Also, do not apply too much pressure to the roller.

Using Spray Paints

Spray-painting stencils is a fairly recent technique. It works especially well for delicate, detailed stencil designs. The spray reaches and perfectly defines the smallest and most intricate stencil cuts, which would probably be lost using the roller or brush techniques. Good for use on walls, spraying is also very effective on furniture, glass, and fabric. The spray creates a myriad of fine dots of color, an effect that helps to retain the lightness and delicacy of a design. This technique is particularly suitable for beginners, although it may require some practice since it is tempting to over-spray, destroying the subtlety of the fine dots and turning the shapes into blocks of solid color.

Spray-stenciled Chest of Drawers

This stencil was taken from a Japanese design but has been used in a random pattern on a white chest of drawers. The intricate, lacelike quality of the design is perfect for spray paint. In some areas the paint appears solid, in others light, giving the design a lively look.

TOOLS & MATERIALS

Acetate stencils

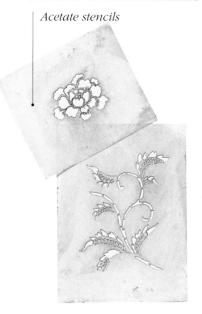

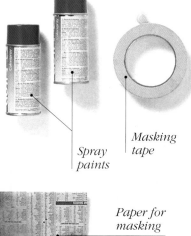

Spray paints

Masking tape

Paper for masking

Piece of board to direct spray

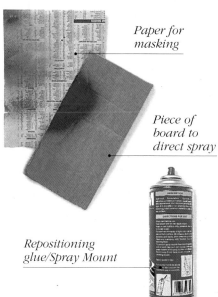

Repositioning glue/Spray Mount

The Basic Technique

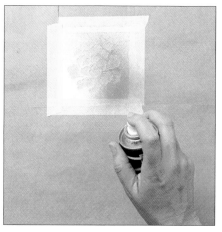

1 Fix the stencil in place using repositioning glue/Spray Mount to prevent the paint from seeping under the stencil. Tape masking paper all around the stencil.

2 Shake the can of spray paint well, then test it on some spare paper. Spray the stencil with a short burst of paint. A small amount of spray creates a delicate array of fine dots.

3 Apply the spray several times to one side of the stencil (inset), allowing the paint to dry for several seconds between each burst. After three or four sprays the paint is quite dense. The contrast between the well-defined shapes on the left and the softer, speckled effect on the right adds interest.

Multi-color Spraying

You can use several spray colors on a stencil to achieve a subtle effect. Blue and yellow in combination, for instance, will appear green from a distance. Be careful, however, not to spray too many colors, or to spray too heavily, or the effect will be muddy. Directing the spray at a piece of board, here corrugated cardboard, will ensure that only the lighter spray falls on the design.

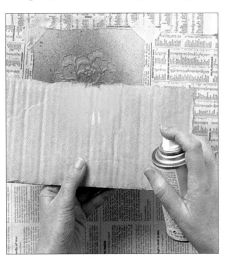

1 *Fix and mask the stencil as in* The Basic Technique *(see p. 111). Spray lightly to give color all over, but spray more heavily in the center.*

2 *Lightly apply a second color. Use a piece of board to mask some of the first color and allow only excess spray to fall on the design.*

3 *Apply a third color. This time use the board mask to direct the paint toward the center of the flower and keep the color light.*

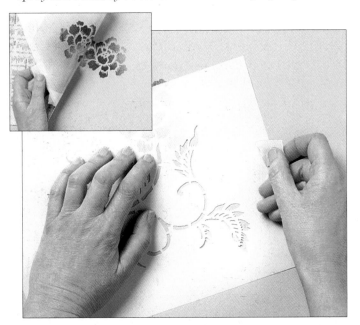

4 *Lift the edge of the stencil to see if the color is working (inset) – if there is not enough of one particular color, replace the stencil and spray lightly again. When the flower is dry, place the leaf stencil next to it. You can see through a new or washed acetate stencil to position it accurately.*

5 *Mask around the stencil and spray your main color – here, green – lightly over the second stencil (above). To create depth, spray more densely in some areas than others. To coordinate with the flower, spray touches of the blue, yellow, and red over parts of the stencil (inset).*

The Finished Design

Multi-color spraying gives a stencil design a sense of depth when viewed from afar (right). This comes from the delicate buildup of different colors that appear to merge when sprayed on. On closer inspection (below right) you can clearly see the variety of colors, and how the spray paint was used to highlight the delicacy of the design. The small spray dots are most apparent at the edges of the outer petals, while the center shows a denser effect.

PITFALLS

If you do not hold the stencil down securely with repositioning glue/Spray Mount, the paint can easily seep under the design, resulting in a blurred image. If too much spray is used, it results in solid color, eliminating the fine dots that add depth and liveliness.

Spraying on Fabric

Because of the deep pile on velvet, it is easiest to make a stencil design on this fabric using the spray technique. Other techniques may leave a thick coat of paint on the surface, flattening the pile, but spray paint does not. Although the paint is quite sturdy and withstands light washing or dry cleaning (a cushion sprayed ten years ago is now faded), it does not last indefinitely.

1 Lightly secure the fabric to a flat surface with masking tape, so that it is smooth and wrinkle-free, but not stretched.

2 Secure the stencil carefully to the velvet, using repositioning glue/Spray Mount. Spray-paint the stencil as described in Multi-color Spraying (see p. 112).

3 The movement of the pile of the velvet can change the effect of the design. At times some colors will seem to disappear, while others look stronger.

Spraying on Glass

Sprays are more effective for stenciling on glass than brushes, sponges, or rollers, because they create an evenly adhering coat. Stenciled glass must always be cleaned carefully since strong abrasives will remove the paint. For a longlasting effect spray on the inside surface of windows, or glass objects.

1 Position the stencil on the glass, using repositioning glue/Spray Mount, then mask the area all around with paper and masking tape.

2 Spray the stencil as in The Basic Technique *(see p. 111). Here, green was used first, strongly in places and more lightly in others.*

3 Apply a second color – here, yellow – in patches. In some areas, use equal measures of the two colors to make a lighter green.

4 Check the color (above) and spray again, if necessary. The finished effect (right) is quite solid, and not easy to see through. A less dense, lighter colored spray would create a semi-transparent effect.

Candle Holder

LEFT *A very small stencil was used on the outside of this glass globe (the stencil has to be tiny to accommodate the curve of the glass). Because masking can be a laborious process, you may want to position several stencils at the same time to accomplish more in one spraying.*

Red Lacquer Chair

BELOW This modern pine chair was sprayed a deep red. Chinese-style designs – figures, pagodas, and trees interspersed with latticework – were then stenciled on in deep gold and bright warm yellow spray paint.

COLOR COMBINATIONS

Dark gold on blue

Red on bright yellow

Dark green on light green

Blue and brown on cream

Velvet Curtain

ABOVE This brown velvet curtain has been stenciled with a design inspired by styles of the 1920s, when velvet printed with flowing abstract designs, often in neutral colors, was especially popular.

Decoupage

Decoupage is the art of cutting out paper designs and applying them to decorate objects, furniture, and walls. Each step requires care to achieve the best results from your design. This chapter combines the practical techniques you need with many inspirational ideas to admire and copy.

Sources of Decoupage

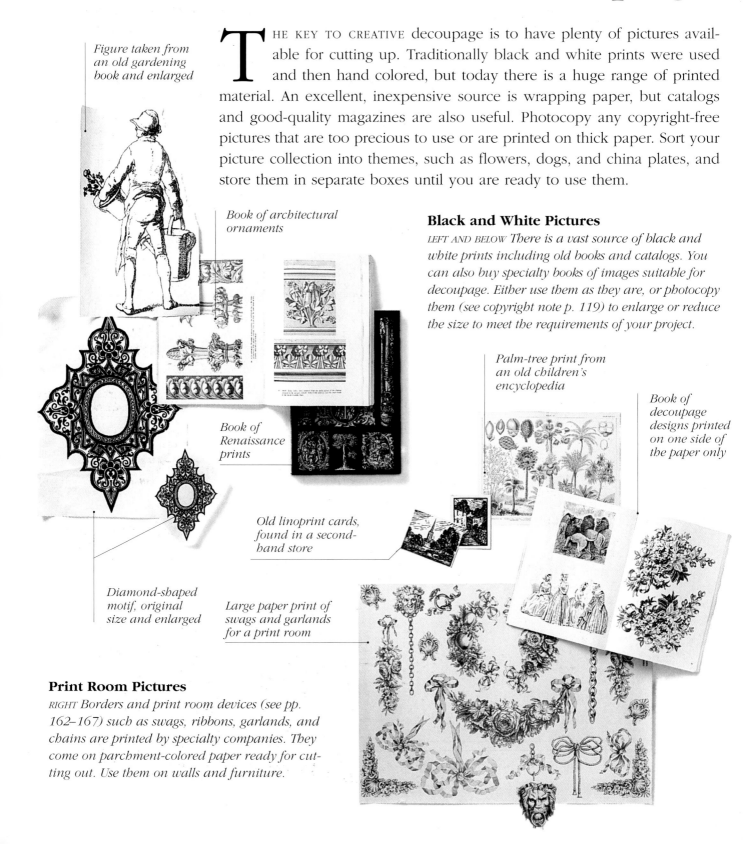

THE KEY TO CREATIVE decoupage is to have plenty of pictures available for cutting up. Traditionally black and white prints were used and then hand colored, but today there is a huge range of printed material. An excellent, inexpensive source is wrapping paper, but catalogs and good-quality magazines are also useful. Photocopy any copyright-free pictures that are too precious to use or are printed on thick paper. Sort your picture collection into themes, such as flowers, dogs, and china plates, and store them in separate boxes until you are ready to use them.

Figure taken from an old gardening book and enlarged

Book of architectural ornaments

Black and White Pictures

LEFT AND BELOW There is a vast source of black and white prints including old books and catalogs. You can also buy specialty books of images suitable for decoupage. Either use them as they are, or photocopy them (see copyright note p. 119) to enlarge or reduce the size to meet the requirements of your project.

Palm-tree print from an old children's encyclopedia

Book of decoupage designs printed on one side of the paper only

Book of Renaissance prints

Old linoprint cards, found in a second-hand store

Diamond-shaped motif, original size and enlarged

Large paper print of swags and garlands for a print room

Print Room Pictures

RIGHT Borders and print room devices (see pp. 162–167) such as swags, ribbons, garlands, and chains are printed by specialty companies. They come on parchment-colored paper ready for cutting out. Use them on walls and furniture.

Original cutout scrap

Colored picture from an old encyclopedia

Pictures from an old children's book

Reprints of Victorian scraps

Catalog picture of a Persian rug

Man's portrait taken from an art catalog

Colored Pictures

LEFT AND BELOW You can use colored pictures from a range of sources, including old books, original and reproduction cutouts. Catalogs are very useful, as the print and paper are of a high quality. Poor paper quality magazines are not recommended, as they are likely to fade or yellow.

Reproduction of an 18th-century painting

Cutout of horse taken from a tapestry reproduction

COPYRIGHT NOTE

Although copyright laws may vary from country to country, you must not sell or photocopy an image that is under copyright to someone else, unless you have their written permission. Look carefully at a sheet of wrapping paper to see a printed note of who owns the copyright. Similarly you can find this information at the front of a book or magazine. Most publishers are happy to give permission, but they will charge you if your design is for commercial use.

Colored Photocopies

BELOW You can get color photocopies made of pictures in books (see copyright note). It is especially useful to be able to enlarge or reduce a picture to the size you require. Over the years the color may fade, so try to apply a varnish that contains an ultraviolet filter.

Enlarged photocopy of painting taken from a book reproduction

Patterned Papers and Postcards

BELOW Wrapping paper (see copyright note p. 119) is readily available and comes in a vast range of designs. If you want to use wallpaper, look for ones that are not too thick. You may need to soak postcards in water or vinegar to remove the thick card backing before applying them (see p. 125).

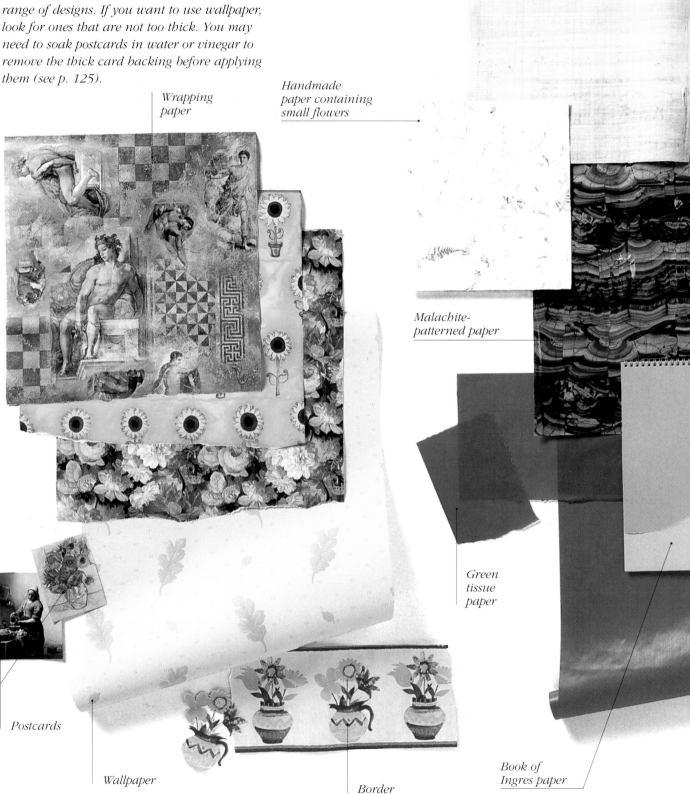

Papyrus

Handmade paper containing small flowers

Wrapping paper

Malachite-patterned paper

Green tissue paper

Postcards

Wallpaper

Border

Book of Ingres paper

Plain Papers

LEFT AND BELOW Plain papers or papers with an overall repetitive abstract pattern are useful for creating your own motifs (see pp. 168–175). Buy them in the form of writing paper and wrapping paper, or from specialty paper shops or art stores.

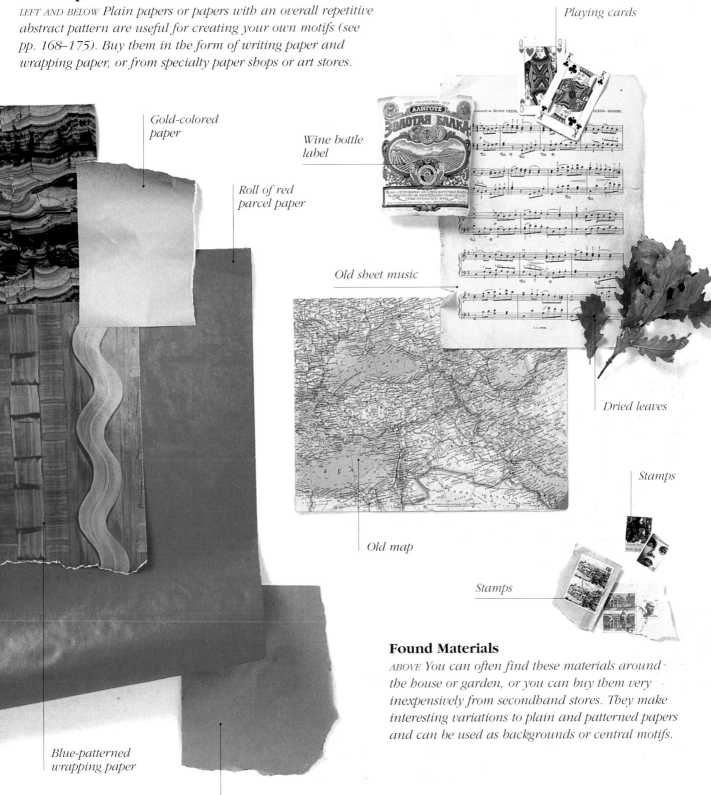

Playing cards

Gold-colored paper

Wine bottle label

Roll of red parcel paper

Old sheet music

Dried leaves

Old map

Stamps

Stamps

Blue-patterned wrapping paper

Brown parcel paper

Found Materials

ABOVE You can often find these materials around the house or garden, or you can buy them very inexpensively from secondhand stores. They make interesting variations to plain and patterned papers and can be used as backgrounds or central motifs.

Tools and Materials

DECOUPAGE REQUIRES FEW tools, some of which you may already have at home. When you begin, improvise by using any available pair of scissors, glues, and brushes. When you are ready to give your work a professional look, you will need to invest in some quality materials, including a craft knife and blades, sharp, pointed scissors, a variety of washable glues, drawing inks, water-base paints, and water-soluble pencils.

Cutting and Sealing Tools

RIGHT A large pair of sharp, pointed scissors is necessary for cutting out big areas. For delicate shapes, use small, sharp, pointed scissors such as sewing or embroidery scissors. A sharp, good-quality craft knife (with changeable blades) is ideal for cutting out intricate and awkward shapes. To seal your paper (see p. 125) before cutting out your motif, use water-base varnish and an acrylic varnish brush.

Sewing scissors

Water-base varnish

Acrylic varnish brush

Craft knife

Large pair of scissors

Embroidery scissors

Glues

RIGHT There are many suitable glues, but make sure you choose a glue that will not mark or leave a stain when you wipe away excess amounts. It must also be thin, so that it does not leave lumps under the paper. The glue should not dry too quickly after contact, since you may need time to adjust your design.

White glue

Starch glue

Gum glue

Flat-ended brush

Sponges, Cloths, Tweezers, and Rollers

BELOW AND RIGHT Once you have glued your picture to the surface, you should remove the excess glue with a damp sponge or cloth. Sometimes you may need to use tweezers to pick up or replace small pieces of paper that shift when you wipe them. On large designs you can also use a roller to flatten the paper and dislodge any air that has become trapped.

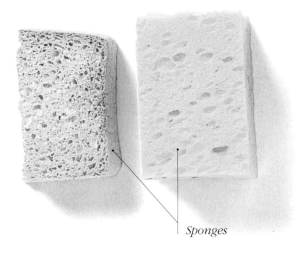

Soft cloth

Roller

Tweezers

Sponges

Coloring Tools and Materials

LEFT AND BELOW Black and white pictures can be lightly colored with drawing inks or any water-base paint. Oil-base paint is only suitable as a base to decoupage on glass (see pp. 150–157) or for painting freehand around paper motifs. You can use shellac or tea to age a black and white print or colored picture giving a light, yellowish-brown effect.

Watercolor paints

Green ink

Green opaque water-base paint

Blue ink

Shellac

Water-soluble colored pencils

Fine artist's brush

Blue opaque water-base paint

Teabag

Preparing Motifs

THE METHOD OF PREPARING your decoupage motif depends on the nature of the design and the object you intend to apply it to. If you are using a photocopy, the paper may be thin and delicate and the inks likely to spread, so it is a good idea to seal the image with water-base varnish before you cut it out. If the image you want is on a postcard you will need to remove the card backing first. Most people prefer to use scissors for straightforward cutting, but for fine, intricate details it is often easier and looks neater to use a craft knife. Try to create a fluid, soft line, since any angular edges will look unnatural. Think carefully about how you cut a design if you are going to apply it to a round object (see p. 127).

Small Scissors

RIGHT A pair of small, sharp scissors would be a good choice here because the man and horse design is broad and not too detailed.

Small scissors

Broad design

Craft Knife

RIGHT Use a craft knife when cutting shapes as intricate as these flowers, especially around the petals.

Craft knife

Intricate design

Border

Postcard

Large Scissors

RIGHT To cut long straight lines use either a craft knife or a pair of large scissors. Small scissors would result in a curving, uneven line.

Large scissors

Postcard

ABOVE To prepare a motif from a postcard, remove the thick card backing by soaking it in vinegar.

Sealing the Motif

If your paper is particularly thin or delicate and likely to tear easily, or the picture surface is fragile and likely to rub off while you are gluing it down, sealing with water-base varnish is a good idea. Test a small area of the picture first to ensure that the inks do not run when you apply the varnish. Use an acrylic varnish brush to apply a single coat of water-base varnish to your picture. Do not overload your brush or apply the varnish too thickly, since the paper may crinkle if it becomes too wet. Allow the varnish to dry completely, for at least 10 minutes.

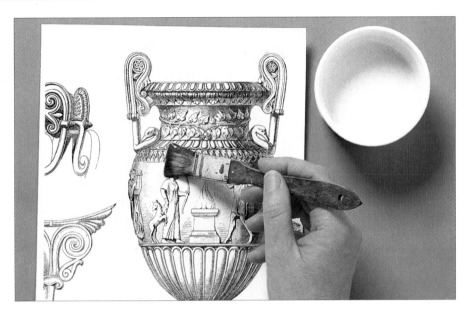

Peeling a Picture off Heavy Card

Some pictures, such as postcards, are too thick to use directly for decoupage, as they require too many coats of varnish to be practical. But postcard pictures are often a good source of decoupage subjects if you remove the card backing, leaving a thin picture, which you can then cut and use.

1 Using a piece of cotton, apply ordinary white vinegar to the back of a postcard until it begins to soften.

2 Starting at the corner, along one edge, peel away the backing. Work patiently, continually applying more vinegar.

3 The wetter the backing becomes, the easier it is to remove. Rub it gently and pieces will roll or pull off easily (right). Allow the very thin picture (far right) to dry naturally before cutting and using.

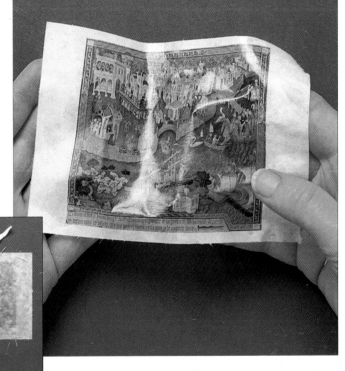

Using Scissors

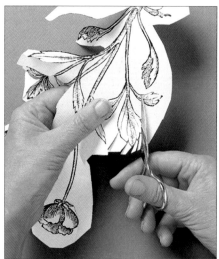

1 Cut off the excess paper surrounding your motif. Here, a picture from a book of flower prints was photocopied (see copyright note, p. 119) and enlarged.

2 Holding your scissors hand still, make snips into the design along lines that face in the same general direction. Move the paper to accommodate small changes of direction.

3 Turn the paper slightly, then cut in the opposite direction, across the snips you have already made. The excess paper will fall away, and the leaf will begin to take shape.

4 You can reach central areas by cutting between parts of the design – here, between the stem and the leaf.

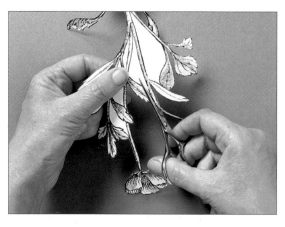

PITFALLS
If you do not carefully follow the outline of your picture, you will end up with visible white edges, as here, around the knees, arms, and feet. These will show up even on a white background. Change your cutting tool to see if this makes it easier.

5 Alternatively, poke the scissors into the central area and cut toward the edges. Take great care when doing this since the position of your scissors may be awkward, causing you to cut off or break delicate outer shapes.

Using a Craft Knife

1 Place the picture on a cutting board. First, make cuts into the design along lines facing in one direction, turning the paper slightly as necessary.

2 Next cut carefully around the shape, working close to the lines but leaving them just visible. Keep the knife in one place while you move the paper.

3 Then cut out central areas, such as those between the stem and leaves in this picture. Tackle delicate parts, such as the stem, last, so that they do not get broken off.

Cutting a Picture for a Round Object

If you have a round object, and a motif that winds all around the object, you will probably need to cut the motif into separate sections and overlap it, in order to make it fit smoothly against the curve. You can hide the places where you have cut the design by cutting along existing lines.

1 Place the design around your object and look to see where you may be able to cut it. Here, the border can be cut approximately every 2in/5cm to fit it around the bowl.

2 Cut along existing lines in the design – here, where the leaves curl to one side about halfway into the design. It is better to make too many cuts than too few.

3 When you glue the design to your round object, overlap the cut edges, making sure that a foreground part of the design overlaps a background part. The end result should be that none of the cuts look obvious.

Staining and Coloring

Tea

BELOW Photocopies are printed on bright, white paper. Stain them with tea to dull the brightness.

Photocopy

Strong tea and teabag

A BLACK AND WHITE MOTIF can be embellished by staining or coloring. Tea stains paper to give it an aged look whereas watercolor paints, inks, and water-soluble pencils are easy to use and can give your motif a subtle or a bright effect. Use a mix of shellac and pigment to give your motif a three-dimensional quality or fill in the background of your motif in a color that matches the base color of the object being decoupaged. Generally, do your coloring before cutting out your motif. That way it does not matter if you go over the edges. However, for painting in highlights and backgrounds it is best to cut and glue first.

Pigment and Paint

RIGHT AND BELOW Embellish classic motifs with subtle highlights and shadows using shellac, pigments, and paints.

Pigment

Paint

Shellac

Ink

Modern motif

Inks

RIGHT The bright clarity of inks gives an old-fashioned look to a modern motif.

Ink

Watercolor paint

Classic motif

Busy design

Paint-brush

Traditional motif

Watercolor Paint

ABOVE AND RIGHT Watercolor paints are light and transparent, suitable for subtly coloring traditional motifs.

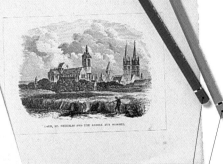

Water-soluble pencils

Water-soluble Pencils

ABOVE Gently color an already busy design with water-soluble pencils.

Staining Large Motifs with Tea

1 Make a tray of tea large enough to dip your picture in without crumpling it. Use a strong tea solution of four teabags steeped in 1pt/600ml water for 20 minutes. Dip the whole motif, sliding it from one side to the other to avoid tidemarks. Leave for a few minutes until soaked.

2 Remove the picture and place flat on newspaper. Dab, not wipe, the picture with a dry, clean cotton cloth to remove excess water. Leave the motif to dry naturally, without putting it near excessive heat.

Staining Small Motifs with Teabags

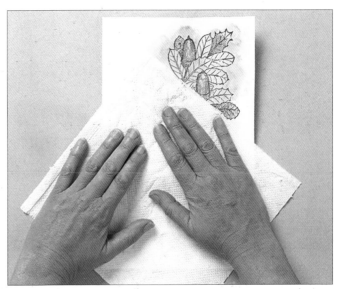

1 Dab your motif all over with a damp, but not dripping wet, teabag to release color from the tea leaves. To keep the color from looking too uniform, squeeze out more tea in some areas for darker color and less in other areas for lighter color.

2 Soak up the excess tea with a tissue, to prevent the paper from becoming waterlogged and crinkled. Allow the motif to dry naturally, without putting it near excessive heat.

Painting in Shadows and Highlights

You can give a black and white motif a three-dimensional aspect by hand painting shadows and highlights. Although this looks impressively difficult, it is merely a matter of following the original design. Try not to fill in the whole drawing, but to give dashes of color that will catch the light.

2 Dip the tip of the brush into some black pigment (inset) and work this into the print with more shellac (right), in the areas already drawn with shadows. Do not obliterate the drawing by using the shellac and pigment too heavily.

1 After sealing (see p. 125) and gluing (see pp. 134–137) your motif to the surface, apply a coat of dark shellac ("button polish" or "garnet polish"), using a soft-haired, flat-ended brush. Let dry for 20 minutes.

3 Using a fine artist's brush, apply beige water-base paint to parts of the drawing that are not in shadow. Add some white to the lightest areas in a few places, to enhance the three-dimensional effect.

4 The print of the urn is transformed into something of great dramatic quality.

Painting in the Background

3 *Varnish the picture to seal it and give it the same tone as your sealed base (inset). Your painted background may look mottled (below) or more solid, if you apply a second coat.*

1 *Here, an intricate pastoral scene was glued (see pp. 134–137) to a base covered in blue water-base paint. Seal the base and picture with water-base varnish (see p. 125) to prevent the paper from being absorbent.*

2 *Resting your hand on a piece of paper to avoid spoiling the work, paint in the background of the picture. Use the same blue that you used for the base. Reach into delicate parts of the design, such as the leaves of the trees, using a fine artist's brush.*

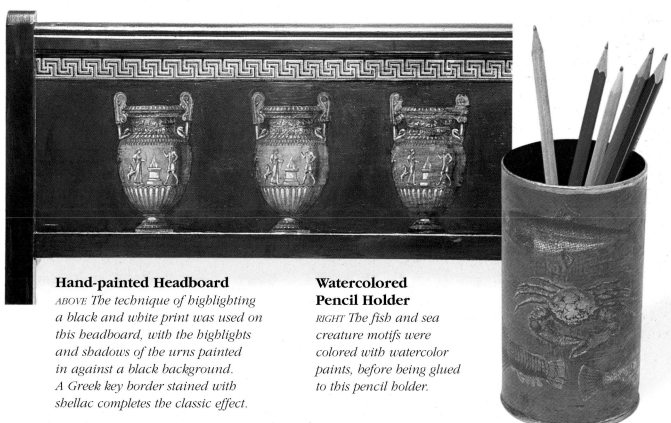

Hand-painted Headboard

ABOVE *The technique of highlighting a black and white print was used on this headboard, with the highlights and shadows of the urns painted in against a black background. A Greek key border stained with shellac completes the classic effect.*

Watercolored Pencil Holder

RIGHT *The fish and sea creature motifs were colored with watercolor paints, before being glued to this pencil holder.*

Gluing

Gluing is a simple process, but if you do it without due care it can create unsightly curled edges, folds, and bubbles. The general rule when gluing is to apply the glue to the surface, rather than to the paper – particularly with delicate pieces – to prevent damaging the design, or saturating the paper, which makes it lose its shape. It is also important to take care when removing excess glue from around your motif and removing air bubbles from underneath the motif, which can be done using a damp sponge, or, for large designs, a roller. Gum-base glues and starch glues are used predominantly in this book, but white glue is equally suitable. When using glue, work in a well-ventilated room.

White Glue

BELOW White glue (also known as PVA) is a strong glue often used for sticking wood together. It is a good glue for using with thick paper.

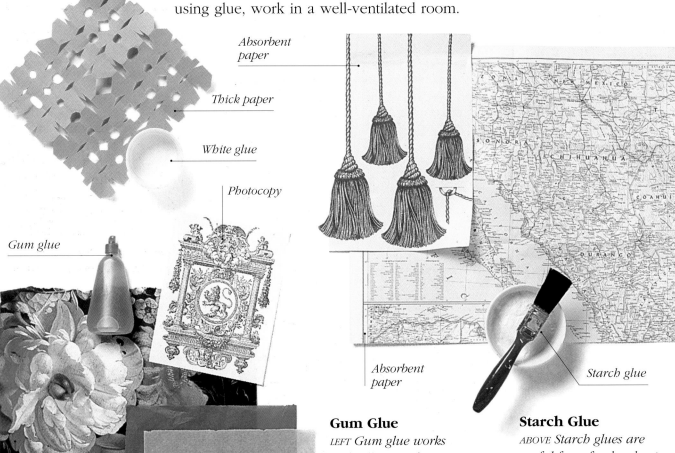

Absorbent paper

Thick paper

White glue

Photocopy

Gum glue

Absorbent paper

Starch glue

Wrapping paper

Tissue paper

Gum Glue

LEFT Gum glue works with all types of paper and often looks brown. It gives you enough time to move your design around but, once dry, the paper adheres permanently.

Starch Glue

ABOVE Starch glues are useful for soft, absorbent papers, and they are white in appearance. They enable you to reposition the paper. Once the glue is dry you can dampen the motif to remove it.

The Basic Technique

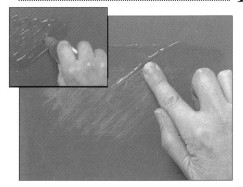

1 *Apply glue to a varnished or painted surface (inset), spreading it with your finger to ensure an even covering.*

2 *Holding your motif in both hands, place it carefully in position. Begin with one side and smooth it down, working across to the other side to help stop air bubbles forming.*

3 *Working from the center out toward the edges, wipe the design gently with a damp sponge or cloth to remove any air bubbles and glue trapped underneath.*

4 *Dab all excess glue from the area surrounding the motif with the damp sponge. Wash out the sponge and repeat. Excess glue can prevent varnish from adhering.*

5 *Pay particular attention to the edges of the design, pressing them down with your fingers. This will help remove any excess glue from underneath and ensure that the corners are firmly in place.*

PITFALLS
To avoid creating folds in your motif make sure the sponge is not too wet. Wipe gently just a few times with the sponge and then dab the surface, so that the paper stretches evenly.

Gluing Delicate Work

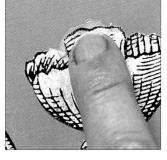

1 Apply glue to the surface as in Step 1 of The Basic Technique (see p. 135). Here, the roots of the flower, the thickest part of the motif, were used to position the motif and were glued down first. Move gradually outward, gluing the next part of the design.

2 Use tweezers to lift delicate parts of the design. These allow you to reposition a piece already glued, without tearing the paper.

3 Press down with your fingers all over the design, to remove excess glue and ensure that no parts remain unglued.

4 Dab the design with a damp sponge. Do not wipe with it, except very gently, because it is too easy to tear the delicate pieces.

5 Rewet the paper so that the fibers soften and the motif becomes flexible and easy to shape. Make use of the stretchiness of the paper, particularly with these long, thin flower stalks by making the flower heads point in different directions. This gives an individual quality to the work, particularly if you repeat the design several times. Once the paper is dry, you can remove any excess glue by wiping with a sponge.

PITFALLS

Take care to remove all the glue from around the edge of your motif, or the excess glue will get dirty. For the same reason, be sure to use a clean sponge to remove glue.

Using a Roller for Large Areas

Some people like to use a roller to flatten down a large motif while it is still wet. Roll from the center out and apply a lot of pressure. Do this before any bubbles form in the paper, or you may make creases.

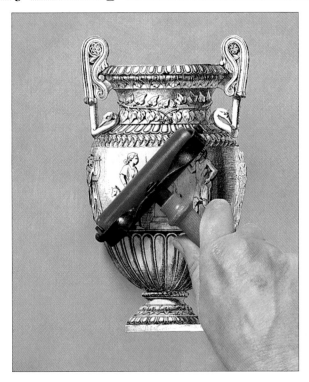

White Glue-covered Frame

BELOW *White glue was used with heavy brown paper to cover this frame. The glue was also used as a varnish.*

Starch-glued Print

ABOVE *Because starch glue was used to position this print, you could reposition it later, if necessary. No varnish was applied, so although the print is perfectly secure, you could take it off the wall with care, by dampening gently with water.*

Gum-glued Box

RIGHT *A simple gum glue was applied to the lid of this box, allowing sufficient time to place the print in the exact position required.*

Varnishing and Finishing

THE AIM IN VARNISHING your decoupage is to be able to pass your hand over the design and not feel the paper. This is why upward of 10 coats of varnish are often necessary, depending on the thickness of the paper and the type of varnish you use. At this stage you can also add decorative touches to your decoupaged objects by coloring the varnish, using crackle varnish, or scratching varnish for an aged effect.

There are two kinds of varnish to consider. Modern varnishes, such as water-base varnishes and specialty decoupage varnishes, dry clear and quickly (see manufacturer's instructions); decoupage varnish needs only 5 or 6 coats. Traditional varnishes, such as oil-base varnish, specialty aging varnish, and shellac, dry with a yellowish-brown tinge for an aged effect. Be sure to work in a well-ventilated room.

Modern Varnish and Pigments

RIGHT Use water-base varnish (also known as acrylic varnish) on its own to give a clear, unobtrusive effect. There are flat and glossy types, although the glossy or satin varnish is the strongest. Apply with an acrylic varnish brush for the best results and spread gently. You can use pigments to color the varnish. Each pigment has a different strength – some are very strong and a little goes a long way. It is best to be cautious, tinting the varnish slightly so that you do not obliterate the motifs.

Red oxide pigment, very powerful

Prussian blue pigment, powerful and bright

Oxide of chromium, powerful and becomes opaque easily

Water-base varnish and acrylic varnish brush

Raw umber pigment, not very strong

Crackle varnish

Cloth for applying oil-base paint to cracks

Oil-base paint

Aging varnish

Strong-haired flat-ended brush

Shellac

Oil-base varnish

Soft-haired flat-ended brush

Traditional Varnishes

LEFT AND ABOVE Use these varnishes to give your decoupaged object a yellow tinge for an aged effect. Oil-base varnish dries very slowly. If you like the quality of oil-base varnish, it is possible to use water-base varnish first and then finish off with an oil-base one. Shellac (sometimes known as "French," "button," or "garnish polish") is based on denatured alcohol/methylated spirits, and dries extremely quickly to give a high gloss to your work. Aging varnish combined with crackle varnish and some oil-base paint will give a distinctly antique look to your work.

Scratching Varnish

BELOW AND RIGHT Scratching water-base varnish with steelwool is another way of imparting an antique look, and helps to give color and patina to the motif.

Dark green-blue water-base paint

Coarse steelwool

Dark red water-base paint

Cotton cloth for wiping clean

Firm-bristled brush

Sponge for wiping off excess paint

Applying Varnish

Here, the three basic varnishes are used to cover three similar motifs, enabling you to see the different kind of finish they provide, and the right brush to use with each to give your work a professional quality.

Water-base Varnish

RIGHT Use an acrylic varnish brush, which is soft but strong enough to push the varnish over the motifs without leaving brushmarks. Try not to overbrush, which will cause streaking marks. Apply 10 coats of water-base varnish or 5 coats of specialty decoupage varnish.

Oil-base Varnish

ABOVE If you apply oil-base varnish directly to paper, you may get a patchy appearance. Avoid this by first applying a coat of water-base varnish. Oil base varnish gives the appearance of age by removing the stark white-ness of the paper. Use a strong-haired flat-ended brush and apply 15 coats.

Shellac

ABOVE Here, the clearest, least colored shellac is being used. Other shellacs known as "button polish," "garnet polish," and "French polish" have more brownish or yellowish tones. Do not overbrush, because shellac dries very quickly and you may cause streaking. Use a soft-haired, flat-ended brush and apply 7-8 coats.

Mixing Pigments into Varnish

1 Apply a layer of water-base varnish all over your motif. You can do this step after applying several layers of varnish or at the first coat, so that you apply more varnish on top.

2 Dip just the corner tip of your brush into the pigment (inset), since you need only a little to stain the motif. Work the pigment into the still-wet varnish. You may require extra varnish in order to work the pigment in.

3 Work a second or third color into the first one. Here, red oxide is being added and mixed with Prussian blue and raw umber. Work quickly.

4 Fill in the background of your motif with other colors – here, green with raw umber. This picture was covered with water-base varnish (right), but you could use oil-base varnish or shellac.

Scratching Varnish

1 Apply at least two coats of water-base varnish to your motif and allow to dry thoroughly for three hours or more, or the varnish will peel off when scratched.

2 Using very coarse steelwool, scratch the surface of the varnish. Try to avoid circular motions, which look unnatural. Scratch in straight lines in all directions, sometimes with long strokes, sometimes with short ones.

3 Using a water-base flat paint, work a firm-bristled brush into the scratch-marks. Use dark-colored paints, such as the greenish-blue and reddish-brown ones used here.

4 Before the paint is dry wipe it off with a damp sponge. The paint will remain in the scratches (right).

Crackle Varnish

1 To make a crackle effect you need two varnishes (an oil-base one and a crackle varnish). Here, oil-base aging varnish is being applied over a motif. You can use a standard oil-base varnish instead. The motif was first sealed with water-base varnish.

2 When the oil-base varnish is partly dry, apply the crackle varnish. If it does not adhere, the oil-base varnish is still too wet. The drier the oil-base varnish, the smaller the cracks will be.

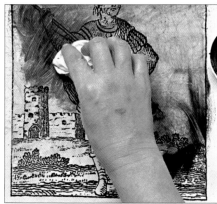

3 The cracks will appear as the crackle varnish dries. Use a hair dryer gently to speed up the process. When dry, rub a dark oil-base paint into the cracks and wipe off any excess with a soft cloth.

4 The finished result gives fine cracks all over the surface (inset), helping to give the picture an antique look. By using ordinary oil-base varnish instead of aging varnish, you get a less brown effect. Cover with a final coat of oil-base varnish for protection.

Pigment and Varnish Lampshade

RIGHT Raw umber pigment was used with a water-base varnish over the flowers and landscapes on this lampshade. This helped to harmonize the prints, some of which are brighter than others.

Scratched-varnish Tray

BELOW The scratched-varnish technique was used on this tray. Black water-base paint was brushed into the scratches over the motif and the terra-cotta paintwork. It was then varnished again, using a water-base varnish.

Shellac-covered Box

LEFT Dark shellac was applied over the Dutch metal leaf on this red box. This gave it a high lacquer shine and deepened the whole effect.

Scratched-varnish Panel

ABOVE This black and white print was lightly colored using watercolor paint (see p. 130), covered several times with water-base varnish, then scratched with coarse steelwool. A dark-colored water-base paint was then brushed into the scratches.

Crackle-varnished Frieze

RIGHT This frieze shelf, or mantelpiece, of decorative jugs, bowls, glasses, and tankards was crackle varnished to bring the design together, although some areas were left bare to highlight the aged effect. Larger patches of dark oil-base paint give the uneven look.

Pigment and Varnish Letter Rack

LEFT This red and green painted letter rack was covered with water-base varnish. Red and green pigments were then worked into the still-wet varnish to create this effect.

Water-base Varnished Frame

BELOW To preserve the strong contrast and clarity of the black and white prints on this frame a specialty decoupage varnish was used to quickly give a high gloss.

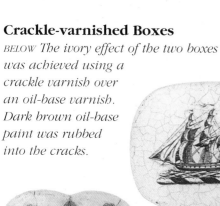

Crackle-varnished Boxes

BELOW The ivory effect of the two boxes was achieved using a crackle varnish over an oil-base varnish. Dark brown oil-base paint was rubbed into the cracks.

Traditional Decoupage

Traditional Headboard

A collection of portrait paintings creates the theme for this headboard. The young girl at the top provides the focus, with the two adults directly underneath giving support. The overlapping background comprises pictures of fabrics, carpets, and landscape paintings.

Decoupage is often closely associated with the traditional 18th century technique of entirely covering a surface by scrupulously overlapping cutouts. At the start of the 20th century artists had adapted this technique to make collages by combining printed pictures, plain paper, fabrics, and three-dimensional objects. Today, precisely positioning motifs is no longer considered important, unless the designs are detailed. The trick to working with detailed cutouts is to set them on the surface, trace the elements to mark their positions, then use the tracing paper to realign your motifs when gluing them down. To ensure the success of any decoupage project, take the time to plan your composition before gluing in place.

TOOLS & MATERIALS

Masking tape for positioning design

Border for scrap design

Landscape for collage

Reproduction scraps and other pictures

Glue

Sponge

Motifs requiring tracing paper for accurate positioning

Tracing paper

Pencil

Scissors

Craft knife

The Basic Technique

1 Release some Victorian-style scraps from their border or cut out some colored pictures, but not in great detail; simply let each scrap form one solid piece of paper.

2 Divide your scraps into large, medium, and small designs – large background pictures, and smaller, focal pictures. Make a loose arrangement of them.

3 Glue down the large background motifs first (see pp. 134–137). Position the medium-sized scraps over the edges of these scenes. Try to visualize where the main picture will go.

4 Now add small scraps, such as butterflies, flowers, or fans. You can cover the whole background or let small areas of background paint show through.

5 To make a neat edge, use a border strip that you bevel, or slant, at the corners. The border should cover any straggling scraps. Cut away any overhanging strips with a craft knife.

6 The main picture gives a focal point to the design but does not dominate it. The five butterflies provide a secondary, unifying theme.

Precise Positioning Using Tracing Paper

1 Cut out a selection of photocopies (see copyright note, p. 119) very carefully, then arrange them in place on your background.

2 Lightly tack down the individual designs with small pieces of mounting putty or tacky tape, to prevent the designs from moving.

3 Fix tracing paper or waxed paper over the design with mounting putty. Trace the design to mark the position of the different elements.

4 Remove a couple of photocopies at a time, and glue them in place (see pp. 134–137). Check their position by realigning the traced design.

5 Remove the tracing paper and wipe off excess glue with a sponge. Varnish (see pp. 138–145).

Making Collage Pictures

1 Gather together a collection of pictures, including one large main picture to use as the background. This could be a landscape, a street scene, or even a house interior.

2 Cut an incision into the main picture. Here, the fish will slot into the background so that it appears to emerge from it.

3 Enhance the three-dimensional look by placing one motif behind another – here, the hare behind one tulip stem and in front of the other.

4 So that the motifs do not overlap the edge of your main design, draw a pencil line down the edge and then cut off any overlaps.

5 Glue all the motifs in position (see pp. 134-137), wiping off any excess glue with a sponge (inset). This scene has a surreal effect because cutouts of varying proportions were used.

Overlapping Trunk

ABOVE *This chest was decorated with overlapping sea creatures and chains against a mottled green background.*

Collage Tray

RIGHT *Figures and landscapes from old master paintings were cut out of an old diary and overlapped on this tray to make a landscape collage.*

Precisely Positioned Cupboard Panel

RIGHT *The inner panel of this cupboard was made to look like shelves containing vases, plates, and jugs. Paper borders were pasted on to imitate the shelves, then the objects were arranged with the help of tracing paper.*

Decoupage on Glass

**Decoupaged
Glass Bowl**

*Medieval scenes were cut
out and glued on the inside
of this glass bowl. Deep
terra-cotta was then painted
over the cutouts to make the
figures and background
appear as one. This simple
yet highly effective technique created the look of an
antique hand-painted bowl.
The inside of the bowl was
varnished for protection.*

DECORATING GLASS using paper offers many possibilities. The basic method of glass decoupage is to glue your cutout motifs to the back of the glass so that you view the scene from the front through the glass. You can either apply opaque oil-base paint over the back so that no light can filter through, or use the light itself; shapes, such as flowers or trees, cut from tissue or other delicate paper can create a translucent effect. A crackle-paint background allows the light to show through, and an arrangement of colored, translucent papers creates a stained-glass effect. Black silhouettes on windowpanes, with no painted background, provide a dramatic look. Alternatively, glue a design to the outside of a glass bowl so you can view it from the inside. The permutations are almost endless. Apply glass decoupage to great effect on bowls, goblets, plates, windows, cabinets, and doors.

TOOLS & MATERIALS

Paper motif

Glue

Oil-base paint

Sponge

Paintbrush

Crackle medium and brush for applying it

Water-base paint

Black paper for silhouettes

Transfer metal leaf

Water-base gold size and brush for applying it

Fine artist's brush

Colored tissue paper

The Basic Technique

1 *Place the cutout paper motif (see pp. 124–127) on the glass pane to determine where you want to position it, either in a central position or slightly further down the glass.*

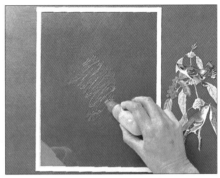

2 *Move the motif to one side and apply a thin, even layer of glue (see pp. 134–137) to the back of the pane (the reverse side from which you will view the design).*

3 *Place the motif, picture side down, on the glass, moving it carefully into position while the glue is still wet. Take care, as thin pieces of the motif can easily break.*

4 *Turn the glass over to check that the motif is correctly positioned. Look for any air bubbles, which are more obvious when you are viewing the design through glass.*

5 *When dry, wipe off all excess glue with a damp sponge (inset). Apply two coats of oil-base paint all over the back of the glass, covering the motif. The finished design shows through the glass (right).*

Sheep Bowl

ABOVE AND LEFT *A naïve-style sheep from a greeting card was glued inside this bowl. Dutch metal leaf was applied behind it, leaving small gaps in which green, black, and white water-base paints were applied.*

Silhouette Plate

ABOVE *Silhouettes of country animals and birds were glued to the back of this glass plate. It was then sprayed with bright red paint to create a strong contrast with the dark animal shapes.*

Stained-glass Door

ABOVE AND RIGHT *The panels of this glass door were given a stained-glass effect, inspired by medieval stained-glass windows.*

African-style Tabletop

LEFT AND ABOVE This glass tabletop uses paper cutouts of people, animals, fish, and birds taken from appliquéd African designs. The background is blue crackle paint sealed with shellac, which is then painted white to give definition to the cracks.

Oriental Vase

LEFT Two Chinese-style paintings of birds were cut from an art magazine and glued to the inside of this vase. A strong green oil-base paint with a little brown was then sprayed on top of the paintings.

Silhouette Lantern

LEFT The silhouette design on this lantern was first sprayed with adhesive spray, then pressed into position on the glass.

Leaf Bucket

RIGHT Leaves taken from a wallpaper design were glued inside this glass ice bucket. It was then sprayed with black vehicle paint.

Decoupage with Freehand Painting

AND PAINTING A SURFACE to create a loosely textured background is a good way to give your decoupage designs an authentic historical look. This approach particularly suits 18th-century scenes, where landscapes often have a slightly blurred look, with more defined painting of people and animals in the foreground. For extra decorative effect you can add in stylized painted clumps of grass or even shadows around the cutout decoupage. You could also adapt the technique to make seascapes and watercolor-style backgrounds (see p. 161). Alternatively, hand painting details on tissue paper decoupage gives a unique, three-dimensional quality.

Hand-painted Chest of Drawers

This chest of drawers was decorated with scenes from 18th-century rural paintings collected from auction-house catalogs. Some of the cutouts were cut in two, to allow for the gap between the two drawers. Grass and shadows were painted on to anchor the images to the background and prevent them from looking as though they are floating.

TOOLS & MATERIALS

Blue water-base paint

Small paintbrush

Off-white water-base paint

Large paintbrush

Dark green water-base paint

Light blue water-base paint

Terra-cotta water-base paint

Paper motifs

Sponge

Glue

Water-base varnish and acrylic varnish brush

Water-base paints

Colored tissue paper

Artist's brush

The Basic Technique

1 Apply blue paint to the top half of the surface. While the paint is still wet work in some white (inset) to create contrasts between pale blue and dark blue areas. Apply the paint unevenly. Be careful not to overbrush.

2 Apply dark green paint, starting at the base of the picture area and working up to meet the sky area in the center. Use white to merge the horizon line, where the green and blue meet (inset).

3 You can add brighter colors in a few places to lift the background. Here a few streaks of bright blue were added to the sky and terra-cotta was added to the ground. Allow to dry for about 5 minutes.

4 Cover the paint with a water-base varnish (either medium-sheen or glossy) to prevent the glue from sinking into the water-base paint when it is applied. Allow to dry thoroughly, which will take about 15 minutes.

5 Position your paper motifs (see pp. 124–127) on the painted background and glue them down (see pp. 134–137) when you are happy with the arrangement.

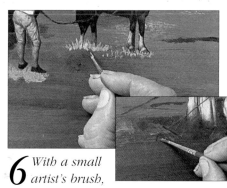

6 With a small artist's brush, add thin vertical lines to simulate grass and dark horizontal lines (with softened edges) to simulate shadows (inset). Apply varnish (see pp. 138–145).

Freehand Painting on Tissue Paper

1 Draw a design of flowers, leaves, or other simple silhouette shapes. Intricate shapes do not work well with fine tissue paper.

2 Transfer your design to different colored sheets of tissue paper, using colors appropriate to your design, either by drawing it again or by tracing it carefully.

3 Cut out the tissue paper design with sharp scissors (inset). Cut out all the pieces before starting to glue them.

4 Tear the flower petals out of tissue paper, to give them a soft edge. Use white tissue paper for the flower centers. Glue the flowers into position.

5 Allow the design to dry for 3-4 hours. It will look messy now, but the design will come to life at the next stage.

6 Using water-base paint and a fine artist's brush, paint circles, spots, lines, and outlines on the flowers and leaves.

7 Here, the bowl was outlined in white, as if the light was coming from the left. The right side was outlined in a darker color, and a smudge of deep blue was rubbed on the side of the bowl to give it depth. Apply several coats of water-base varnish (see p. 140) for protection.

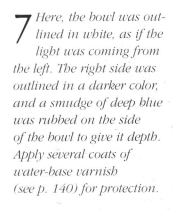

8 The translucent nature of the tissue allows you to "see" through the foliage and flowers, giving the design a three-dimensional quality.

Persian-style Box

LEFT AND BELOW Photocopied. Persian paintings were arranged on a background of pale blues, greens, and mauve. Small tufts of grass and flowers were hand painted between the horsemen, and lines around the box lid.

Classical Box

ABOVE Hand-painted pearls were added around the edge of this frottaged and decoupaged box.

Leaf and Berry Curtain Pole

ABOVE AND LEFT Strips of tissue paper were glued around this curtain pole. The berries were painted with dark shadows and highlights to give them shape, and the leaves with a central vein for definition.

Fish Tray

ABOVE AND RIGHT Black and white pictures of fish were glued to this dark blue and black tray. Lines and dots of color in blue and off-white water-base paint were added in between to create a stylized water effect.

The Print Room

THE TRADITION OF print rooms began in 18th-century Great Britain. Etchings or engravings were glued to the wall and complemented by borders, swags, ribbons, and garlands. The print room loosely copies the traditional arrangement of real paintings and the rococo fashion of stucco decoration on the wall. Try to use original black and white prints, rather than photocopies, and buy accessories, such as borders, ribbons, and swags from specialty stores. Before embarking it is essential to find a group of prints that work together, perhaps on a theme such as ancient Greece, plants, or birds. Alternatively, you can adapt the method to a single print, framed and pasted on a wall or small object.

The Print Room

This entire room was decorated with prints and borders. The tasselled ropes were glued in different positions, adding a lively elegance. A frieze was added to the top of the wall around the room.

TOOLS & MATERIALS

Spirit level

Metal ruler

Clear plastic ruler

Protractor triangle

Pencil

Small scissors

Large scissors

Cutting board

Craft knife

Plumb line

Print and print accessories

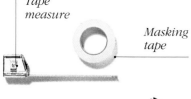

Tape measure

Masking tape

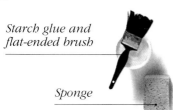

Starch glue and flat-ended brush

Sponge

Preparing a Print

1 Using a large protractor triangle or a T-square, draw a pencil line around the print, making certain the corners are right angles – old prints are often not straight. Here, equal space was left on all sides of the single, central motif. Be careful not to get finger-prints on the print, which will show up later.

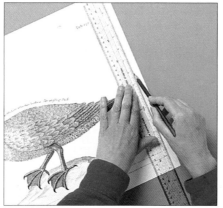

2 Draw a second frame, about 1/4in/6mm outside the first. You can do this with an ordinary ruler, but it is easier with a clear plastic ruler – align one of the ruler lines with your inner pencil frame and draw another pencil line downward.

3 Find the central point of each line by measuring it, and make small pencil marks. Do not mark the print inside the inner frame.

4 Cut along the outer pencil line on all sides of the print, using large, sharp scissors or a craft knife. To give your print an aged look at this stage, stain it with tea (see p. 129). Prepare all the prints in the same way before proceeding to the next step.

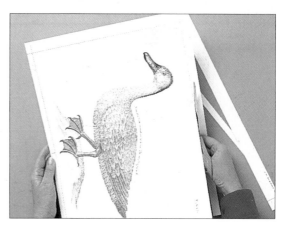

Framing a Print

1 Place small pieces of masking tape all around the underside edge of the print so that the sticky side of the tape is uppermost.

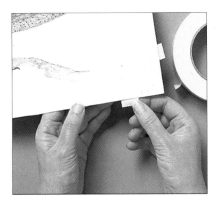

2 Choose the border design for your print. Cut sufficiently long lengths of border so that it overlaps at each corner. Secure the border to the masking tape, aligning it with the inner pencil line.

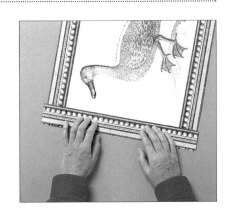

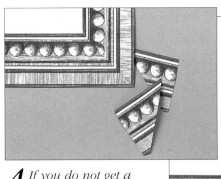

3 Place a metal ruler diagonally from corner to corner of the overlapping borders. Using a craft knife with a sharp blade, cut along the ruler. Don't worry if you cut through to the print.

4 If you do not get a good corner match (inset), you can hide it, using corner tabs (right).

Adding the Framework

1 Place together border strips in the corner of the room, until you have covered the full height of the wall (inset). Using a spirit level at right angles to the corner strips, draw a pencil line along it at the correct height for the chair rail.

2 Apply glue to the back of the paper chair rail. Using the pencil line as a guide, press the paper chair rail onto the wall across the entire room.

3 Within the area below the chair rail, mark out panels in pencil. Cut out and glue down border strips to delineate the panels.

Measuring

1 *Using small pieces of masking tape lightly fix the prints in position on the wall. Adjust them until you are satisfied with the grouping. Lightly tack down ribbons, ropes, swags, and other details. Mark the top center of each print lightly in pencil on the wall.*

2 *Remove each print one by one and use a plumb line – a weight attached to string and used to determine verticality – to accurately mark their central positions on the wall.*

Finishing

1 *Remove the border strips and immerse the print in a tray of cold water for a minute or so (inset). Remove and place upside down on spare paper for gluing. With a flat-ended brush, apply a generous coat of starch glue.*

2 *Position the print on the wall, aligning the central mark on the print with the central mark on the wall. Use a plumb line to make sure that the line is vertical. Dab with a damp sponge to flatten the print.*

3 *Glue ribbons, swags, and other details in position, and add the border frames. Although print rooms are not traditionally varnished, you can add one or two coats of varnish for protection (see p. 140).*

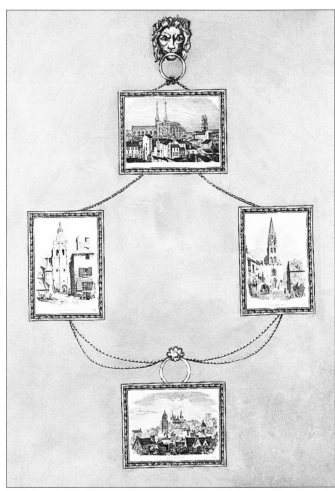

Print Room Walls

*ABOVE AND RIGHT An old
print of palm trees was
combined with floral swags
and a central architectural
device hung with flowers
(above). Prints of French
villages were brought
together using ropes,
against a toning beige
background (above right).
A rich, deep green paint
picked up the greens in
these botanical prints,
while the traditional print
room borders helped to
harmonize the colors and
unify the group (right).*

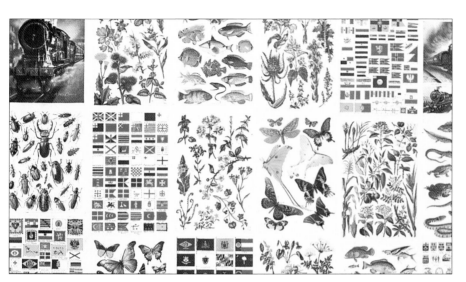

Continental-style Print Room

LEFT These prints from an old children's encyclopedia have varied themes, but work well together. They were cut to regular sizes and pasted close together.

Two Wastepaper Baskets

RIGHT AND BELOW The black wastepaper basket has a central motif and complementary borders. The cream wastebasket was decorated with borders and swags, and then crackle varnished (see p. 143).

Key Box

ABOVE A homemade 1930s' hand-printed woodcut found in a secondhand store was used on this small key box. The strips were cut from classical borders to match the dark main motif.

Garlanded Hat Box

RIGHT This hat box uses decorative devices that are traditionally used between the images of a print room, as well as borders. It has a lining of marbled paper.

Classical Box

ABOVE This small round box with its circular border has a classical print taken from an old book as its central motif.

Making Your Own Designs

Stencil Motif Container

A Victorian-style stencil was used as a template for the motif on the front of this dried flower container. It was cut out of marbled paper and glued to a frottaged background in terra-cotta and green.

YOU CAN USE PLAIN and patterned papers to make your own designs, either freehand or with a template. Use a stencil as a template, or draw around a photograph to make a simple silhouette. Cut around a single motif on concertina folded paper to make a repeat pattern in a border. You can simply create your own designs in paper by cutting geometrical shapes out of folded paper, to reveal diamonds, triangles, and stars when you unfold it. Achieve a symmetrical motif by cutting half a design into a single folded sheet of paper, or create a completely individual effect by cutting circles, spirals, and slots into a solid motif. Keep your cut shapes simple and you can achieve some delightful results with which to decorate boxes, panels, drawer fronts, and lamp shades.

TOOLS & MATERIALS

Wrapping paper

Stencil

Scissors

Craft knife

Pencil

Silhouette photograph

Tracing paper

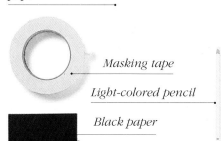

Masking tape

Light-colored pencil

Black paper

Wrapping paper

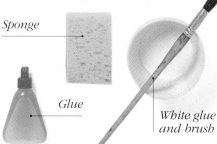

Sponge

Glue

White glue and brush

Using a Stencil

1 Place your stencil design on your paper. Draw around the outside of the stencil card with a pencil. Here, a simple stencil design was used with wrapping paper.

2 Following your pencil marks, cut out the card shape. Because the paper has an abstract repeating pattern you can repeat the motif any number of times.

3 Place the wrapping paper on top of the stencil card and turn both card and paper over.

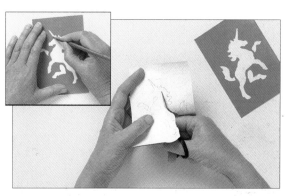

4 The white side of the paper will now show through the stencil shape. Draw around the stencil shape (inset), then cut it out (above).

5 To help position the design correctly, draw around the stencil shape on the surface where you want to glue it. Apply glue to the surface inside the pencil marks (see pp. 134–137).

6 Press the paper pieces into position (inset). In the final design (above) the two unicorns were placed facing each other.

Silhouettes

1 Silhouettes can come from a wide variety of sources, including the examples shown here: a book of traditional silhouettes (some of them are very complicated), a bird book, black and white drawings, a children's cutout, a colored picture, a leaf, and a photograph of someone in profile.

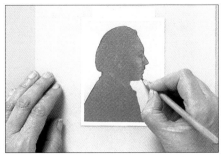

2 Using masking tape, secure some tracing paper over your silhouette. Trace the outline of your silhouette, using a very sharp pencil.

3 Turn the tracing paper over and draw over the traced line using a light-colored pencil that shows up against the black paper.

4 Turn the tracing paper over again and secure it to a piece of black paper with masking tape. Using a sharp pencil, trace over the design one more time.

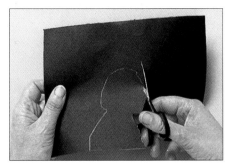

5 The light colored pencil marks will transfer to the black paper. Cut out the silhouette, following the light colored pencil lines.

6 Use this silhouette for any decoupage project. Here, the stark black paper cutout is on a colorful patterned background that lifts the design.

Folding Paper to Make a Repeat Border

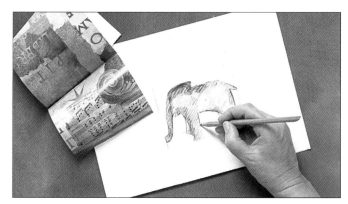

1 Draw a design with a solid center and narrow extensions on each side – the trunk and tail of the elephant – to line the border. Draw a rectangle around the motif so that on either side the lines touch the narrow extensions of the motif. Cut out the rectangle to use as a template.

2 Cut a strip of patterned wrapping paper. Position your template on the back of the strip at a far edge. Mark in pencil the edge of the template. Position the template next to the first mark and mark again. Repeat until you have the desired amount of repeats. Fold the paper along these lines into a concertina shape.

3 Cut out the drawing and place on top of the folded paper strip. Trace around it. Make certain that the trunk and tail extend to the edges of the paper so that they will link the border.

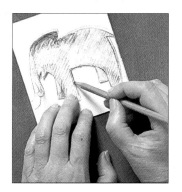

4 Hold the folded paper strip in one hand and, with your other hand, cut through all the layers at once following your outline. The trunk and tail touch the edge of the concertina strip so you do not snip into them and they hold the border together.

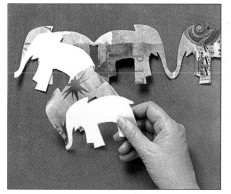

5 Pull the strip open to reveal a row of elephants holding trunks and touching tails. This asymmetrical design results in pairs of elephants, facing each other and back-to-back.

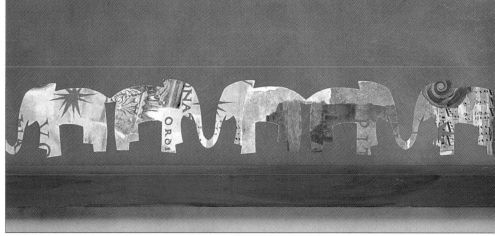

6 Glue the border (see pp. 134–137) to a strong-colored background. The random patterns and colors of the wrapping paper add interest to the design and break up the solid shape of the elephants.

Making a Geometric Design

1 Fold your paper – here, handmade paper, but you can use any paper – in half, and in half again. Fold it in half one more time. You can do more folds if your paper allows.

2 Cut notches along all four edges of the paper. Alter the length and width of the notches to give variety to the design.

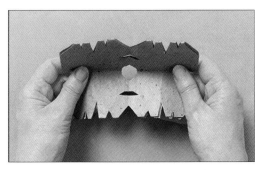

3 Open the paper out once. This will reveal that there are areas of the paper where there are no holes.

4 Fold the paper in the opposite direction from the direction you have just unfolded – here, lengthwise – and cut more notches, altering the length and width, along the new fold.

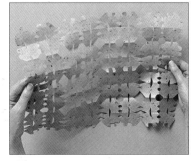

5 Unfold the paper carefully to make sure you have cut into all the areas. You can make an enormous range of patterns.

6 Glue the cutout to your surface (see pp. 134–137). You can use any type of glue. Here, white glue was used.

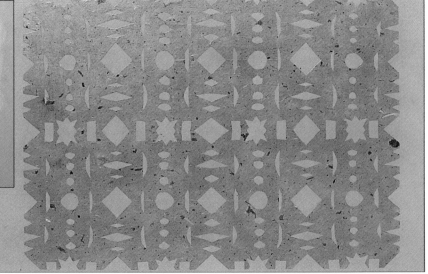

7 Paint over the design with white glue (above) to help flatten the paper. Work from one side to the other to prevent the paper from stretching. The white glue gives a strong, shiny finish (right).

Scissorwork

1 The red fish and the green dancing figures shown here are examples of Chinese scissorwork designs. The black and white bird design comes from Poland and the design with the figures and flag from America. These traditional ways of cutting paper to make designs might be inspiration for your own projects.

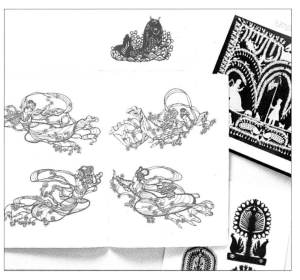

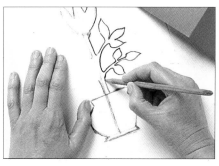

2 Draw a simple symmetrical image, such as the plant here. Draw a line down the center of your picture. Lay a piece of tracing paper over your drawing and trace the right half of the design.

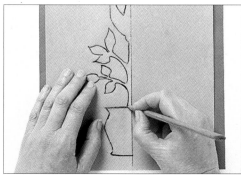

3 Turn over the tracing paper and transfer the half design to colored paper by retracing over it, so that the original pencil line shows up.

4 Fold the colored paper in half along the edge of the design. Cut out the design, using sharp scissors and following the pencil lines.

5 Unfold the cutout, to get a symmetrical design. Glue to your background (see pp. 134–137).

Cutting Shapes

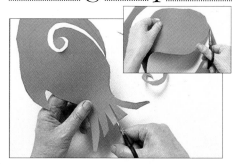

1 Draw a simple fish shape on colored paper, then cut it out with a pair of scissors (inset). Cut into the design from the edge to make spirals and a fringed edge for the tail.

2 Using a craft knife, carefully cut out slots and circles within the solid body of the fish.

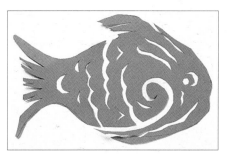

3 This fish comprises simple cutout shapes. Starting with broad, basic designs and gradually cutting more intricate shapes is good practice for more complicated designs.

Symmetrical-patterned Cupboard

LEFT AND BELOW The panels of this cupboard were decorated with symmetrical designs that were made by cutting plain and decorative wrapping paper along a fold.

Silhouette Box

BELOW AND RIGHT Inspired by ancient Greek pottery, this silhouette of a profile was cut from black paper set against the orange lid of this box.

Stencil Motif Box

BELOW A stencil of a horse was used as a template here. The pieces were cut out of carpet designs taken from magazines and glued to this box.

Repeat-patterned Chest of Drawers

LEFT AND BELOW Folded and cut borders, based alternately on birds and flowers, were used on the drawers of this blue and green chest.

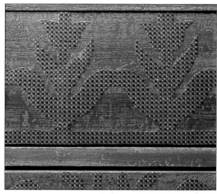

Silhouette Mirror

ABOVE Silhouettes of leaves from different trees were cut from black paper and glued against a background of wrapping paper that also has a leafy pattern, to cover the frame of this mirror.

Geometrical Tabletop

RIGHT This wood tabletop was decorated with paper folded and cut into geometrical and other abstract shapes that were glued to patterned wrapping papers.

Wood Finishes

Use the techniques in this chapter to add interest to wood and embellish the natural beauty of its grain. A wonderful range of wood is available, each having different types of grain—some smooth and narrow, some coarse and wide, some knotted, and others curled.

Fine artist's brushes (0 to 4 sable or sable mixtures are best)

Pencil

Tools and Materials

ANY WATER-BASE PAINTS, ALSO KNOWN as acrylic paints, can be used when painting on wood and it is important to use good quality brushes, especially when doing intricate hand painting. Working with a brush that does not have a good point or is loose will result in poor work since the brush is not controllable. Techniques that use paint on wood include hand painting and stenciling designs which can then be embellished using metal leaf. Other techniques involve imitating a wood grain with brushes, combs, and graining rollers, revealing wood under a painted surface, or distressing the painted wood using wax and steelwool.

Source material photocopy

Stencil

Stencil brushes

Water-base Paints

BELOW *There is a basic range of traditional colors used for painting on wood. The colors tend to be biased toward cool blues and greens as a foil to the warmth of the wood. Spots of warm pink, pale orange, off-white, and creamy ocher could also be used.*

Painting Designs on Wood

ABOVE *Collect pictures of possible designs for transferring onto your surface, taking inspiration from old painted furniture and designs found on fabric and china. Use fine artist's brushes, 0 to 4 sable or sable mixtures, for painting intricate designs on wood, and stencil brushes when stenciling on wood (see pp. 92–93).*

Pale gray-blue

Middle blue

Warm raspberry-pink

Gray-green

Middle green

Pale terra-cotta

Woodgraining

BELOW AND RIGHT There are specialty tools you can buy for Woodgraining (see pp. 70–71), but some of these can be improvised at home. Combs, for example, can be made from plastic tiles, and household brushes can be used instead of a flogging or dragging brush. However, the specialty transparent water-base glaze is essential. When this is mixed with paint it gives it a translucent quality and stops it from drying out, giving you more time to complete the technique.

Water-base glaze

Water-base paint

Comb

Flogging brush (a dragging brush can also be used)

Flat-ended paintbrush

Oval-shaped paintbrush

Revealing Wood Under Paint and Painting and Distressing

BELOW Use paint stripper to reveal wood under a painted finish or masking fluid as a variation. To achieve a distressed effect, rub your surface with wax before painting over it, then rub away the paint in places using steelwool. Crackleglaze can also be used to create a similar, antiqued effect (see pp. 210–213).

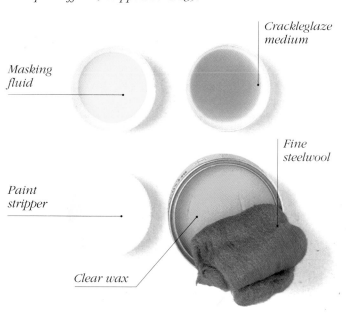

Masking fluid

Crackleglaze medium

Fine steelwool

Paint stripper

Clear wax

Applying Metal Leaf

BELOW Another way to embellish wood is by applying metal leaf (see p. 208). Metal leaf, here Dutch metal leaf, which imitates gold, is not as expensive as it might look. It is applied with a special glue called gold size.

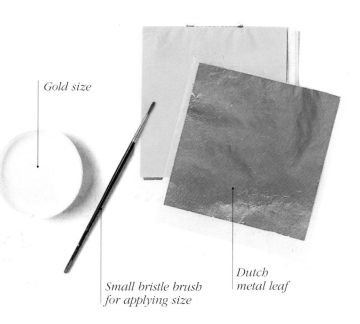

Gold size

Small bristle brush for applying size

Dutch metal leaf

Using Homemade Stains

Pigment-stained Birch Containers

These traditional Shaker-style birch pieces are stained using warmed pigment paste. A second color was applied to the edges and central areas of the tray.

I N THE PAST, WOOD HAS BEEN stained with many different materials. The easiest to use is a stain made with pigments, which is said to be the stain used by the Shakers. Van Dyck crystals (see p. 182) are still popular today for their richness of color, ease of use, and economy, and ferrous sulfate (see p. 182) also makes a useful and economical stain. The strength of your stain depends on the ratio you use of powder to water, but remember that soft, light wood generally changes color more readily than dark, harder wood. Stains are absorbed by wood and so work well to enhance the interesting, expansive grains of woods like walnut. These woods are usually expensive, but you can buy them as veneers at a fraction of the cost.

TOOLS & MATERIALS

Spoon

Pigment

Old saucepan

Cotton cloth

Van Dyck crystals

Van Dyck stain
and paintbrush

Protective
gloves

Ferrous
sulfate

The Basic Technique

Pigments come in varying strengths. The depth of color you obtain depends on the strength of your pigment and the type of wood you use. Experiment to find the ratio of pigment to water that you prefer.

1 Using an old saucepan (it will stain), add 1 part pigment to 5 parts water or your preferred ratio. Heat, stirring, until it begins to boil and has a thin, pastelike consistency.

2 Remove the saucepan from the heat and allow to cool slightly. Dip a cotton cloth into the mixture while still warm and rub well into the wood, using pressure.

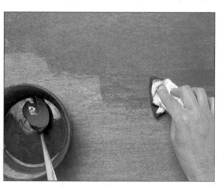

3 Using a clean cotton cloth, rub all over the surface to remove excess pigment. The grain of the wood should become increasingly apparent.

4 The surface should dry within a few minutes. If the color is not strong enough, apply a second coat of the warmed pigment paste.

5 With a dampened absorbent cloth, wipe over the surface again to remove all loose pigment.

Van Dyck Crystals

This is a rich brown staining medium bought in crystal form and dissolved in warm water. It was originally made from the soft outer husks of walnuts, but is now more likely to be made from an extract of peat bogs. The color depends on the strength of the stain, as shown on these pine blocks (right). These contain (left to right): 1 part Van Dyck crystals to 15 parts water; 1:10, 1:5, 1:2. A recommended strength is 1:5.

1:15   *1:10*   *1:5*   *1:2*

1 *Wear protective gloves since the mixture is very strong and can stain the skin and nails. Combine 1 part Van Dyck crystals with 5 parts warm water. Mix well.*

2 *Apply a generous layer of stain to the wood. Do not allow it to dry in between strokes since any overlap may create darker areas.*

3 *Wipe off any excess stain using a clean dry cloth and allow the stain to dry completely.*

Using Ferrous Sulfate

This is the chemical name for an iron compound that you can use to turn wood from gray to an inky-black, ebony color. It also turns oak silvery gray and gives walnut, which is naturally yellow, a gray tone. It only affects wood that contains tannin, such as oak, walnut, and sycamore.

1 *For a very strong, dark stain, mix 1 part ferrous sulfate with 10 parts cold water and stir well. Test the mixture on a small, hidden area of your wood to judge the strength you require.*

2 *Paint on the stain and allow it to soak in. Here, it was painted on a piece of walnut. Wipe off any excess with a damp cloth (inset).*

3 *Here, the color of the wood has changed from a hot, almost orange color to a cooler gray-brown. It will have darker and lighter patches, depending on the grain of the wood.*

COLOR COMBINATIONS

*Red oxide
on cherry*

*Antwerp blue
on maple*

Blue and Green Stool

ABOVE Blue stain (1 part pigment to 5 parts water) was applied all over the stool using a cloth. When dry, green stain was applied using a brush around the edge of the seat.

Banded Bed Headboard

BELOW 1 part ferrous sulfate to 20 parts water was painted in a band around the edge of this bed head-board, together with a thin, delicate line to emphasize its shape.

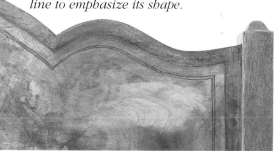

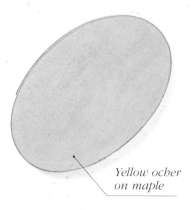

*Yellow ocher
on maple*

Stained Candlestick

ABOVE This oak candlestick was stripped of paint, leaving the wood looking dark, but dull. It was stained with Van Dyck crystals (1 part Van Dyck crystals to 5 parts water) to strengthen and warm it, leaving the raised bands in the original color.

PITFALLS

You must remove varnish from old pieces of furniture (see p. 14), or the stain will not reach the wood that is still covered by the varnish, as here. Carefully look at and feel the surface of your wood since varnished areas will be slightly shinier and smoother.

*Burnt umber
on birch*

Using Modern Stains

THERE ARE TWO TYPES of modern stain, both of which are available ready-made from hardware stores and are relatively easy to use. Water-base stains come in bright, light, modern colors as well as wood colors. These stains work particularly well for soft woods and light-colored woods. Oil-base paints are available in mainly brown wood colors and produce strong, deeply penetrating stains, which work best with darker-colored woods. You can use modern stains on any wood to showcase its natural grain. You should bear in mind that the color of the wood will affect the eventual color of the stained work. A yellow wood, for instance, with a warm blue stain will result in a cool green-blue.

Stained chair
This new pine chair was first stained in a raspberry-pink water-base stain. Over this a dark green stain was applied and then rubbed in places to reveal the pink (above). Several colors were used on the carved cockerel including red and ocher (right).

TOOLS & MATERIALS

Water-base stains

Cotton cloth

Bristle brush

Stencil brush

Stencil

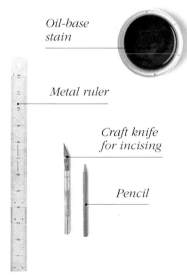

Oil-base stain

Metal ruler

Craft knife for incising

Pencil

The Basic Technique

1 *Using a bristle brush, apply water-base stain to the required areas. Don't worry if the colors appear bright; they will deaden when dry.*

2 *Rub off the excess stain with a clean, dry cotton cloth. Use a fresh piece of cloth for each area, so that you do not spread the stain.*

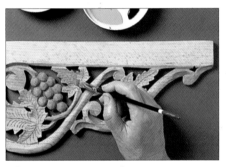

3 *Using a clean bristle brush, apply a second color of stain to other areas. If you are staining a carved object – as here – use a small brush so that you can reach into the crevices.*

4 *You can also apply color by dipping a cloth into some stain and wiping it over the raised areas. The cloth will not reach the recessed areas, creating a lively blend of colors.*

5 *Paint a coat of brown water-base stain over the surface to tone down the object. If you use a third coat, the stain will look dark and opaque. Varnish, wax, or oil the finished work (see pp. 138–145).*

Using Two Colors

Here, the second color is applied in spots, but you can also apply a second color all over a stained surface to create a two-toned effect. Wood soaks up more stain in some areas than others so in some places the first color will be more apparent, and in others the second color will be dominant.

1 Rub all over the wood with medium-grade sandpaper. This breaks up the surface slightly, helping the stain to penetrate.

2 Wearing protective gloves, soak parts of a cotton cloth or sponge in the first stain – here, a water-base stain – then wipe it over the wood, following the direction of the grain. Avoid drips. Keep working into a wet edge to prevent two coats of stain from building up in any area, which would give a darker color.

3 Using a clean cloth, wipe off excess stain, again working in the direction of the grain. This will make the color of the wood appear lighter. Allow to dry for about 20 minutes.

4 Apply the second stain with a cloth or sponge, either in specific areas or all over. The two colors could contrast – here, green and red. Or, if the first color is bright, you can apply a muting color, such as brown or white.

5 Wipe off excess stain using a clean cloth, taking care to wipe the spots only, so that they do not smudge. Wiping off a lot of the second stain with considerable pressure will result in more of the first color being seen.

Stenciling with Stains

You can use water-base stains in the same way as paints to create patterns with stencils. Firmly attach the stencil to the surface using either masking tape or repositioning glue/Spray Mount. You want to be sure that stain doesn't seep underneath the stencil. You can stencil directly onto wood or onto stained work, but more than two layers of stain will become opaque.

1 The secret of stenciling with stains is to use a very small amount of stain on the brush. Dip a stencil brush in the liquid, dab it on some spare paper to remove the excess color and apply – here, to the flower.

2 Apply two or more colors to the rest of the stencil, using a clean stencil brush each time. Here, the different parts of the design were colored separately, but there could be more overlapping to create a blended effect.

3 To give depth, add a second color on top of the first in places. Here, we are adding to the flower center, but you could do it at the edge of the petals.

4 Lift up part of the stencil to check that the colors are working well and make any adjustments you consider necessary.

5 To give the stencil a coherent look, a little of the red and some blue was used on the leaves. With stenciling, which leaves a "gap" between parts of the design, you avoid the fuzzy edge created by painting colors back-to-back.

Making Patterns with Stains

To make a pattern using stains, you need to incise the wood with a craft knife. This prevents the stain from flowing along the grain and enables you to use two different colored stains side by side, without the risk of them spreading.

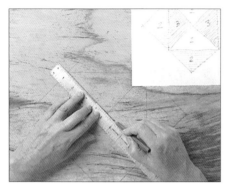

1 Draw your design on the wood using a pencil and ruler. Geometric patterns are easy to do.

2 Using a very sharp craft knife and a metal ruler, incise along the lines to a depth of 1/16in/2mm.

3 Using water- or oil-base stain, paint the design. Use a small bristle brush to reach the corners easily without spreading the stain. Use a larger bristle brush over bigger areas.

4 Apply a second color in the same way as the first. There is no need to wait for the first color to dry before doing this. You can then apply other colors in the same way. Protect the surface with a coat of varnish, oil, or wax on water-base stain or shellac on oil-base stain (see pp. 138–145).

Checkered Table

ABOVE *A geometric pattern with a three-dimensional effect was drawn and scored into this tabletop. Three shades of oil-base stain were then painted on using a small brush.*

Two-Tone Frame

ABOVE *This simple pine frame had a black oil-base stain applied using a small brush to part of the raised molding. A lighter oil-base stain was applied to the frame using a cloth.*

Stained Kitchen Cabinet Door

LEFT The color of the central panels was first deepened with diluted water-base stain. The stencil was then applied using the same stain at full strength. A black stain was applied to the molding.

COLOR COMBINATIONS

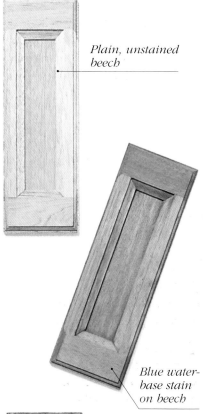

Plain, unstained beech

Blue water-base stain on beech

Swedish-Style Bench

BELOW AND RIGHT This new pine bench was stained using a water-base stain applied with a cloth. On the backrest a stencil was applied in water-base stains using stencil brushes.

Brown water-base stain on beech

Red water-base stain on beech

PITFALLS

Applying water-base stain can be tricky, especially over large areas, since the stain dries quickly. Wipe drips off quickly or they become impossible to remove, and try not to load the brush, cloth, or sponge with too much stain.

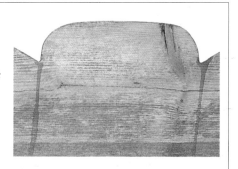

Fuming a Pattern

It is easy to fume a pattern on wood by using the tannin content of tea, especially on a wood that does not already have a high tannin content. Paint a strong solution of tea (see p. 191) inside a traced and incised design. Be sure to make enough tea to cover your whole design – 1 cup would be plenty for a small design. After fuming, the wood will appear darker where you have painted it with tea.

1 Trace in pencil a design that has large, bold shapes and is not too intricate. For a light wood, rub a dark pigment or pencil onto the back of the design; for a dark wood use pale-colored chalk or pigment.

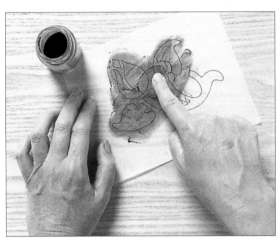

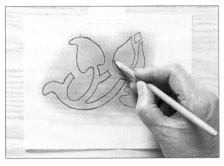

2 Transfer the design to the wood by tracing over it again. Where you apply pressure, the pigment will leave a mark on the wood.

3 To prevent the tea from seeping through the grain of the wood onto areas where you do not want it, incise carefully with a sharp craft knife along the lines of the design, to a depth of at least 1/16in/2mm.

4 Paint the tea solution inside the cut marks with a fine brush (inset). Do not paint right to the edge of your design, but allow the liquid to soak up to it. Place the object in a container with ammonia sulfate overnight (see p. 191). Where the tea solution was applied, the wood will darken and the design will stand out.

The Basic Technique: Bleaching

You can lighten dark and colored woods using specialty wood bleaches (household bleach will not work). A strong, effective bleach comes in two parts – or three parts including a neutralizer – and there are many proprietary brands. Wear protective gloves and a face mask when using wood bleach.

1 Apply Part A of the two-part bleach with a special vegetable-fiber bristle brush, which the bleach will not destroy. Leave for 5–10 minutes, or as directed on the instructions.

2 Apply Part B of the two-part bleach. The bleached surface will almost immediately begin to bubble (inset).

3 When the surface has dried, after a few hours, you will see how light the wood has become. To make it even lighter, repeat Step 2.

4 When the color is light enough, wash over the wood using the neutralizer suggested by the manufacturer. Allow to dry.

5 Wash the whole area with water to remove any traces of the neutralizer. Be careful not to over-saturate the wood.

6 The wood now appears lighter all over. Here, the oak has changed from a medium brown to a warm, pale yellow. If Part B was reapplied, the wood would be even whiter. You can now either use the bleached wood as it is, or you can stain it in some way.

Bleaching a Pattern

You can make simple patterns or designs in wood, such as on a tabletop or sections of furniture, using the two-part bleach. The bleach has a tendency to spread, working its way along the grain of the wood. To prevent this, use a craft knife to lightly incise the outline of the pattern into the wood.

1 *Draw a simple pattern in pencil directly onto the wood. If the design is too intricate, especially on hardwood, it will be difficult to cut.*

2 *Using a sharp craft knife, incise the wood along your pattern to a depth of at least 1/16in/2mm, to prevent the bleach from seeping along the grain.*

3 *Using an old brush, since the bleach will whiten the hairs, apply Part A of the bleach (see p. 193). Allow to dry for 5-10 minutes, or as instructed.*

4 *Apply Part B of the bleach, painting it in the same direction as the grain. Do not paint right to the edge of your design, but allow the liquid to soak up to it. When the surface has dried follow Steps 3–6 of The Basic Technique: Bleaching (see p. 193).*

5 *Here, the result is a precise, geometric pattern but you can easily create a more flowing design by applying both parts of the two-part bleach in dots.*

Incised and Bleached Frame

RIGHT This oak frame was incised with a craft knife, making various geometric shapes. Parts of the frame were then bleached using the two-part bleach, to a near-white color, to create a sharp contrast with the dark, unbleached wood.

COLOR COMBINATIONS

Fumed/natural bleached old pine

Fumed/natural/bleached new pine

Fumed/natural/bleached walnut

Fumed/natural/bleached mahogany

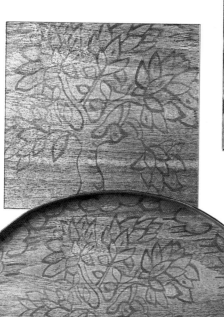

Bleached Tray

LEFT This walnut tray was painted with masking fluid in the shape of a tree and then bleached. When the masking fluid was removed, the tree motif remained unbleached. The whole tray was then covered with an oil-base varnish.

Bleached Table

RIGHT First the varnish was removed from alternate slats of this table. These were then bleached to a light, slightly pink-honey color, to create a striped effect.

Penwork

Penwork Box

This wooden box has penwork decoration, using both The Basic Technique (see p. 197) and the Dark Background technique (see p. 198). The curved top, made of soft plywood, was sealed with four coats of sanding sealer to prevent the ink from running into the grain.

THIS TRADITIONAL TECHNIQUE is a method of allowing finely grained woods to contrast with an opaque layer of decoration in ink. India ink which is black and sepia – a warm, brown ink – are the most commonly used. Although the work looks meticulous and time-consuming, it is actually done quite quickly, once you have done the tracing. It is simply a matter of drawing around the design and filling in the spaces with ink, using mapping pens, calligraphy pens, or fine artist's brushes, all of which are available from art supply stores. You can use waterproof drawing ink or ordinary writing ink, which is more transparent and is not waterproof. Penwork is suited to pale, rather yellowish woods, since they contrast well with the darker ink. It is important to first seal the wood (see p. 14–15).

TOOLS & MATERIALS

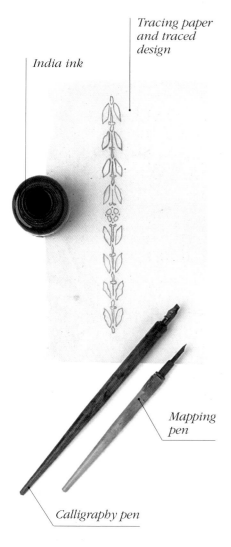

India ink

Tracing paper and traced design

Mapping pen

Calligraphy pen

Fine artist's brush

Pencil

The Basic Technique

1 *Trace a design. It is best to use simple repeated patterns which you can photocopy and, if necessary, enlarge to suit your project.*

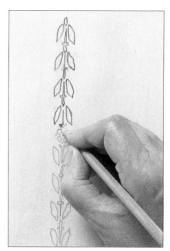

2 *Having sealed the wood (see pp. 14–15), transfer the design onto the surface using pigment and pencil.*

3 *Dip the nib of a mapping pen into the ink. On spare paper, remove any excess ink so that drips do not occur. First draw around the shapes, then fill in the centers.*

4 *Draw lines to separate different parts of the design. Practice first – raise the ruler slightly, load the nib with ink, then draw a line straight up until the ink runs out. Reload and start again, slightly overlapping the line where you finished.*

Dark Backgrounds

Trace and transfer a design onto your sealed wood surface (see pp. 14–15). Draw around the outline using a mapping pen. Instead of filling in the design, you fill in the background using a fine artist's brush. Apply a second coat of ink for a more solid background. Do not overload the brush with ink.

Using Diluted Ink

By using diluted ink (start with a ratio of 1 part ink to 1 part water), you can achieve a softer effect. Fill in the outline of your design with both diluted and undiluted ink to create shadows and depth.

1 Dilute the ink, testing it on spare paper or wood and adjusting the strength if necessary. Using a fine artist's brush, apply the diluted ink to areas of the design, such as the central areas of the leaves and flowers, as here.

2 Add lines in undiluted ink, using a mapping pen to give definition to the design. Here, lines were applied to make leaf veins and add shadows.

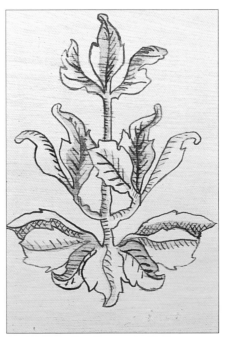

3 The finished effect includes cross-hatching, where you draw ink lines in opposite directions to emphasize dark areas.

PENSTROKES

Penwork was traditionally done with a fine mapping pen, but you can also use a calligraphy pen. Here, an angled, square-ended nib is used to create a wide variety of patterns, ranging from small diamond shapes to angular and wavy lines.

Small diamonds

The upward stroke is a thin line, the downward stroke is thick

The downward stroke is a thin line, the horizontal stroke is thick

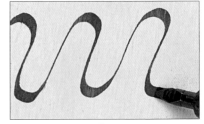

A looping line widens and narrows

Marquetry-style Corner Cupboard

RIGHT AND BELOW This pine corner cupboard has a design based on an antique chair decorated with marquetry work. The central brown stripe occurs naturally in the wood's grain. The penwork was done in India ink.

COLOR COMBINATIONS

Blue ink on poplar

India ink on poplar

Green ink on beech

Sepia Frame

LEFT The leaves and designs on this plain, modern pine frame were hand drawn using sepia-colored drawing ink. It was then coated with oil-base varnish.

1930's-style Bowl

RIGHT The penwork on this small bowl made of wood from the rubber tree was done in green writing ink and brown drawing ink. The bowl was varnished using oil-base varnish to protect it and make it washable.

India and red ink on beech

Gilding

Gilding can be used for a wider range of applications than you might think. Shimmering bronze powders or loose metal leaf will add a contemporary sparkle or an aged look to furniture, walls, and a variety of smaller items around your home.

Tools and Materials

BRONZE POWDERS ARE very fine powders that come in a range of metallic colors. Despite their name, they are not in fact made of bronze. The "silver" powder is actually aluminum, while the rest are varying mixtures of copper and zinc. Traditionally they are used over oil-base size, either in a solid pattern or sprinkled on top to create a glittery varnish. You can also use them in wax, to stencil or to add finishing touches with a thin gold line. By adding the powders to varnish, you can create paints for fabrics, walls, or furniture. Bronze powders produce less shine than metal leaf, but they are generally easier and cheaper to use.

Rich pale gold

Pale gold

Light gold

Orange gold

Medium gold

Deep copper

Antique copper

Crimson copper

Copper

Fire copper

Silver

Bronze Powders

ABOVE AND RIGHT *Bronze powders are available in a wide range of colors, including several golds, from light yellow modern golds to dark golds and older, reddish golds. There are also several copper colors, ranging from modern to old coppers and the more spectacular crimsons.*

Greenish-gold

Reddish-gold

Pewter

Silver

Copper

Medium gold

Metallic Waxes

LEFT *Several colors of ready-made metallic waxes are available from art supply stores. For other colors you can mix your own by combining clear wax with a bronze powder.*

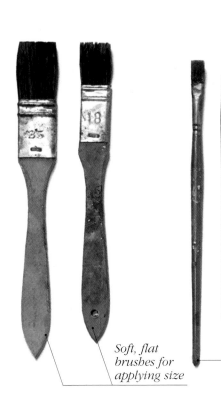

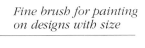

Fine brush for painting on designs with size

Brushes

Use a soft brush for applying size, so that you can apply it smoothly. For brushing on and working with bronze powders, use a nylon brush that is soft-bristled. For applying wax, use a stenciling brush.

Stenciling brush

Soft, flat brushes for applying size

Stiff, soft brush for brushing on and sprinkling bronze powders

Varnish and Size

BELOW *The water-base varnish and size (bottom and below left) are white, but after application dry clear. The oil-base size (below right), is the color of clear honey when liquid and becomes transparent on application.*

Face Mask

Because of the very fine, powdery nature of bronze powders, it is advisable to wear a face mask while working with them, especially on time-consuming projects.

Oil-base size

Water-base size

Water-base varnish

Wax

This neutral wax is a whitish color that becomes clear when spread thinly. Other clear waxes may have a yellow or orange tinge. These are fine for use with gold and copper powder, but with silver you need to use a neutral wax.

Palette knife for mixing powders into wax

Bronze Powders

AFTER METAL LEAF, BRONZE POWDERS create the shiniest and most metallic effect. Traditionally you use bronze powders by dusting the fine particles onto gold size so that they adhere. You can also sprinkle the powder over a tacky coat of oil-base size or brush it onto a stenciled or hand painted design. Do this technique in a draft-free environment, because bronze powders are extremely fine and liable to blow around. You should also wear a face mask for protection against breathing in dusty particles. The size will not tarnish the metals, but you should coat your finished work with oil-base varnish for a long-lasting effect. Early American settlers used bronze powders with stencils, often placing designs of fruit and flowers in gold on a dark-colored background. Your own design does not have to be complicated – a simple arrangement of spots and dots can be highly effective.

TOOLS & MATERIALS

Dark gold bronze powder

Copper bronze powder

Medium gold bronze powder

Small bristle brush for dusting on bronze powder

Water-base size and fine brush for applying it

Large, soft bristle brush for removing loose bronze particles

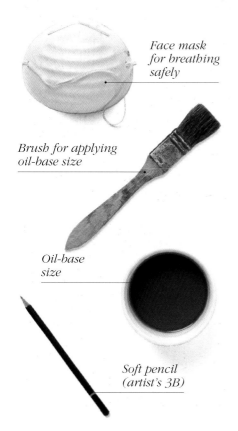

Face mask for breathing safely

Brush for applying oil-base size

Oil-base size

Soft pencil (artist's 3B)

The Basic Technique

1 Paint the surface evenly with a coat of oil-base size. Oil-base size (see p. 203) will dry and become clear on the parts of the surface that are not covered by the bronze powders.

2 When the surface is tacky, pick up a little bronze powder on a small bristle brush and tap the brush gently to make the powder fall onto the surface.

3 A second, third, or even fourth bronze powder may be added to give the effect more life. For a different look, apply powders while the oil-base size is wet rather than tacky. This causes the powders to spread slightly. Or you can dust the powders solidly in some areas to give variation.

Loose Metal Leaf

METAL LEAF – copper, aluminum, silver, gold or Dutch metal – that comes without a sheet of waxed paper backing is called loose leaf. Because loose leaf is very light, it crinkles and tears easily, making it harder to apply than transfer leaf; even a draft can affect the laying of the leaf. We do not demonstrate the use of loose real gold leaf in this book, because it is too difficult for the novice gilder to handle. Despite these concerns people often prefer loose leaf to transfer leaf, because it costs less and works well on carved surfaces (which transfer leaf does not), and for the distressing technique (see pp. 210–213).

Gilded Chair

This chair was painted off-white, with very dark brown paint applied in the recesses. Loose Dutch metal leaf was then applied, allowing the background paint to show through at the top of the chair and on the legs. The metal leaf was covered with an oil-base varnish.

TOOLS & MATERIALS

Paint

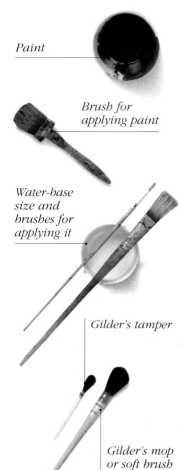

Brush for applying paint

Water-base size and brushes for applying it

Gilder's tamper

Gilder's mop or soft brush for dabbing metal leaf

French chalk or talc for dusting fingers

Sheet of loose metal leaf

The Basic Technique

1 *Paint your surface (see p. 203). Allow to dry. You can use either water- or oil-base paint, flat or glossy, although oil-base paints can take up to two weeks to dry.*

2 *Apply a coat of size. Water-base size is best for the beginner, since it remains tacky indefinitely giving you more time to complete your work.*

3 *To prevent the metal leaf from sticking to your fingers, dust them lightly with French chalk or talc before handling it.*

4 *Take a sheet of loose metal leaf in both hands and lower it carefully into position, starting at one edge and easing the rest into place. If a sheet tears, try to match up the edges as closely as possible.*

5 *Using a gilder's mop or a soft brush, smooth the metal leaf onto the surface. Dab it down, rather than wiping it, so that it does not tear before adhering properly.*

6 *Continue to cover the surface, slightly overlapping sheets of metal leaf. Wipe away any excess leaf with the gilder's mop, saving excess to fill gaps (see p. 208).*

Filling Gaps

1 *To fill gaps, holes and tears in the surface, pick up a small excess piece of metal leaf, using a gilder's mop or a finger dusted in French chalk.*

2 *Press the piece into the gap, using your fingertip or the gilder's mop. If it does not stick, add more size to the exposed surface and reapply the metal leaf.*

3 *When all the gaps are filled, gently brush away any excess metal leaf. Brushing too briskly will break the metal leaf into pieces too tiny to use.*

PITFALLS

Brushmarks, grit, or hair from a brush all show up under loose metal leaf. Begin with a smooth, dust-free surface and use good, soft brushes.

Applying Loose Metal Leaf in Selected Areas

1 *Paint a design on your surface, either freehand or using a stencil, with any water- or oil-base size. Allow it to dry.*

2 *Tear pieces of metal leaf off the sheet and dab them onto the design, pressing down all over to make sure they have stuck.*

3 *Wipe away all excess metal leaf. Using a soft brush, rub firmly over the entire design to make certain that the leaf is adhering.*

Distinctive Vase

ABOVE *Irregular rectangles were painted in water-base size over the surface of this blue china vase. The rectangles were then overlaid in a varied pattern of loose copper, aluminum, and Dutch metal leaf.*

Applying Loose Metal Leaf to a Carved Surface

1 Using a small brush to reach the intricate areas, apply a coat of water-base size, making sure the whole surface is covered. Allow to dry.

2 Tear the metal leaf into small enough pieces to cover the surface in sections. Don't use a whole sheet or the metal leaf will break.

3 When the size is tacky dab the leaf pieces gently onto the surface with your fingers, pushing them into position around the carving.

4 Rub the surface with your fingers to bring out the carving's details. Use a gilder's tamper for more intricate areas.

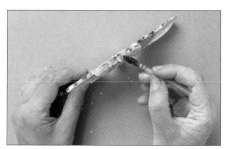

5 To cover up any holes, push excess metal leaf into position with the gilder's tamper.

6 Brush off excess metal leaf and fill in any remaining gaps. You can now color the surface, distress it, or simply leave it as it is. Because aluminum leaf was used here, the surface does not need varnishing.

Distressing

O NE OF THE DELIGHTS OF old gilded objects is the way the metal leaf has worn away in places to show the color underneath. You can re-create this look in your own gilding by rubbing wax – either good quality furniture wax or beeswax – gently over the metal leaf with very soft steelwool. This breaks the leaf up into tiny pieces, leaving traces of metal on the painted surface. The technique does not have to look traditional; for a more contemporary look use brightly colored backgrounds, or rub through the metal leaf to make shapes. A coarser steelwool dipped in either turpentine or water will create a more pronounced effect – a good technique for large objects.

Distressed Cupboard
The emerald green base was coated with oil-base size. Sheets of transfer copper leaf were applied with spaces in between, making a diamond lattice pattern. The surface was then distressed with medium-gauge steelwool dipped in turpentine and protected with oil-base varnish.

DISTRESSING IN CLOSE-UP

Applying the metal leaf with accuracy is difficult. Once the leaf has stuck, you cannot move or reposition it, so you need to make a virtue of any fault that you have created. Scratch away at areas where the gaps are too large or too small.

TOOLS & MATERIALS

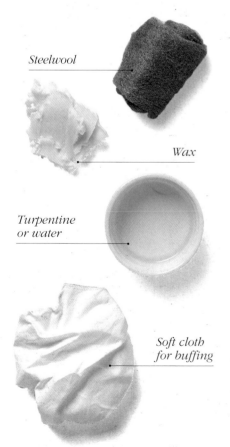

Steelwool

Wax

Turpentine or water

Soft cloth for buffing

The Basic Technique

1 After painting the surface and covering it with loose or transfer metal leaf (see p. 207), rub over it with very fine steelwool dipped in wax. Use clear or colored wax.

2 Using a non-waxy part of the steelwool, rub over the leaf to remove parts of it. Any areas of the leaf that have folded or crinkled will produce a more obvious mark.

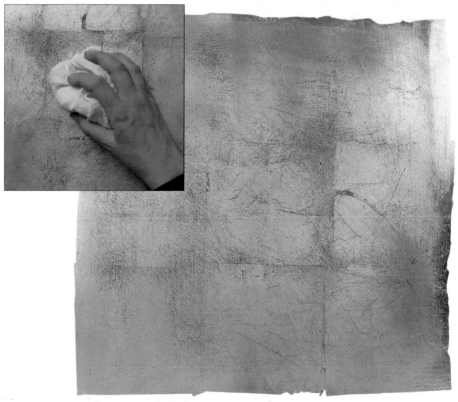

3 Leave the wax to harden for about 10 minutes, then buff to a soft sheen (inset). The wax initially dulls the metal leaf, but when buffed gives it a soft, mellow shine like old gold (above).

Making a Pattern in the Leaf

1 Make patterns by rub-
bing hard in certain
areas to reveal the color
underneath. Here fine
steelwool dipped in clear
wax was rubbed in lines
over aluminum leaf.

2 After finishing the design, rub
wax all over until you cannot see
any areas of unwaxed leaf. Leave to
harden for 10 minutes.

3 Buff the entire surface of the
patterned and waxed leaf with
a soft cloth (above) to give an overall
sheen (below).

ALTERNATIVE

You can combine two different
colors of metal leaf, using one
on top of the other. Here,
Dutch metal leaf was laid over
a terra-cotta surface, then an
aluminum layer was applied
randomly on top, leaving some
gaps. The whole effect was
then rubbed back with soft
steelwool to show glimpses of
both the Dutch metal and even
the terra-cotta base.

Distressed Drawers

*BELOW These drawers were covered
with several bright colors and overlaid
with transfer Dutch metal leaf. The
surface was rubbed back to create
flower patterns and then buffed.*

COLOR COMBINATIONS

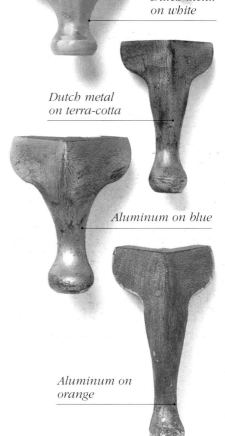

Copper on greenish-blue

Dutch metal on white

Dutch metal on terra-cotta

Aluminum on blue

Aluminum on orange

Highlighted Frame

ABOVE *Dutch metal leaf was laid over the terra-cotta base of this frame. It was rubbed back with fine steelwool and dark wax, removing some areas almost completely and leaving others shiny gold. The surface was then buffed.*

Distressed Bureau

ABOVE *This dark blue desk was overlaid with loose aluminum leaf, rubbed with wax using steelwool, then buffed. Where the leaf tore, more of the blue can be seen.*

Antiqued Candlestick

ABOVE *This candlestick has a terra-cotta base color, with Dutch metal leaf on top. To achieve the effect of an old, worn object, clear wax and the finest steelwool were used to rub away some of the metal leaf. The surface was then buffed.*

PITFALLS

If paint or size is not applied evenly and with care, brush-marks may be left on the surface that will become more apparent when the metal leaf is rubbed with steelwool and wax. This detracts from the paint-and-metal leaf effect.

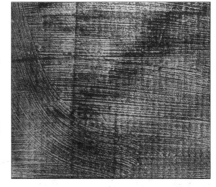

Suppliers

In the United States
Jerry's Artarama
5325 Departure Drive
Raleigh, NC 27616
Toll-free: (800) UARTIST (827-8478)
Phone: (919) 878-6782 (in NC)
Fax: (919) 873-9565
Email: uartist@aol.com
Website: www.jerrysartarama.com

Michaels
850 North Lake Drive
Suite 500
Coppell, TX 75019
Toll-free: (800) MICHAELS (642-4235)
Website: www.michaels.com

Dick Blick Art Material
P.O. Box 1267
Galesburg, IL 61402-1267
Toll-free: (800) 828-4548
Phone (309) 343-6181 (Int.)
Toll-free fax: (800) 621-8293
Email: info@www.dickblick.com
Website: www.dickblick.com

Pearl
1033 E. Oakland Park Blvd.
Fort Lauderdale, FL 33334
Toll-free (800) 221-6845
Toll-free fax: (800) 732-7591
Email: Pearlsite@aol.com
Website: www.pearlart.com

Jo-Ann
2361 Rosecrans Avenue
Suite 360
El Segundo, CA 90245
Toll-free: (800) 525-4951
Fax: (310) 662-4401
Email: customercare@joann.com
Website: www.joann.com

In Canada
Curry's Artist's Materials
Head Office & Warehouse
2345 Stanfield Road, Unit 3
Mississauga, ON L4Y 3Y3

Toll-free: (800) 268-2969
Phone: (416) 798-7983
Toll-free fax: (877) 772-0778
Email: info@currys.com
Website: www.currys.com

Loomis & Toles Art Stores/Omer DeSerres
(Vancouver to Halifax locations)
Head office:
254 Ste. Catherine Street East
Montreal, QC H2X 1L4
Toll-free (800) 363-0318
Phone: (514) 842-6637
Toll-free fax: (800) 565-1413
Fax: (514) 842-1413
Email: support@loomisartstore.com
Website: www.loomisartstore.com
www.omerdeserres.com

In the United Kingdom
annieSLOAN practical style
117 London Road,
Oxford OX3 9HZ
Phone: 01865 768666
Website: www.anniesloan.com
Paints and interior decoration products, courses on painting and interior decoration

Bailey's Paint
Griffin Mill Estate, London Road
New Stroud, Thrupp
Gloucestshire GL5 2AZ
Phone: (01453) 882237

Interior Affairs
Decorative Furniture,
Painting and Accessories.
6 The Grove
Westbourne
Emsworth
Hampshire PO10 8UJ
Phone: (01243) 389972

Creative Decorating
Maranatha, Whitbrock
Wadebridge
Cornwall PL27 7ED
Phone: (01208) 814528

Acknowledgments

Special thanks to:

      Geoff Dann (photographer) and his assistant Gavin Durran
      Steve Wooster (designer)

Thanks also to the following people for guidance and advice or providing items to work on:

Bennison Fabrics
      Joanna Casey
      Eri Hz. Heiliggers
      Relics of Witney, Bret Wiles, Chris Walker and Ray Russell
      Stuart Stevenson
      Jane Warwick
      David Wessex
      Whistler Brushes
      Nicola Wingate-Soul

The Annie Sloan range of paints, varnishes and glazes are used in this book
(see list of suppliers for more information).

Index